ON NOT FOUNDING ROME

On Not Founding Rome

The Virtue of Hesitation

STEVEN SCHROEDER

CASCADE *Books* · Eugene, Oregon

ON NOT FOUNDING ROME
The Virtue of Hesitation

Cascade Books
An Imprint of Wipf and Stock Publishers
199 W. 8th Ave., Suite 3
Eugene, OR 97401

www.wipfandstock.com

ISBN 13: 978-1-60608-610-0

Cataloguing-in-Publication data:

Schroeder, Steven, 1954–

    On not founding rome : the virtue of hesitation / Steven Schroeder.

    viii + 162 p. ; 23 cm. Includes bibliographical references and index.

    ISBN 13: 978-1-60608-610-0

    1. Philosophy. 2. Theology. 3. Metaphysics. I. Title.

BR115 .P7 S32 2010

Contents

Acknowledgments

Part of chapter 3, "The Virtue of Hesitation," appeared in an earlier form as "No Goddess Was Your Mother: Western Philosophy's Abandonment of Its Multicultural Matrix," *Philosophy in the Contemporary World* 2:1 (1995) 27–32.

Chapter 6, "Real Presence," first appeared as "Anne Conway's Place: A Map of Leibniz," *The Pluralist*, 2:3 (2007) 77–79. Used with permission of the Univer-sity of Illinois Press.

Chapter 7, "God and the World," appeared in an earlier form as "A Little Madness," in *The Existence of God*, Edited by John R. Jacobson and Robert Lloyd Mitchell, 245–57. Lewiston, NY: Mellen, 1989.

Chapter 9, "The Shape of the City," first appeared as "A City in which Violence is not Necessary: Notes Toward a Philosophy of Nonviolence," *Philosophy in the Contemporary World* 10:2 (2003).

PART ONE

On Not Founding Rome

I

Counting Cats

I offer this book as an invitation to philosophy in the context of "Western" ideas: it is a hybrid—part cookbook, part atlas, part guidebook.

Cookbooks work best when they are used creatively. Simply following a recipe might produce something edible; it might even produce a tasty dish. But the simple follower of recipes is not likely to come to mind when you think of good cooks or master chefs. The good cook may start with a recipe, but she or he is not likely to stop there. When good cooks try to tell you how to cook, they often resort to concepts like a pinch of this and a dash of that. You learn what a "pinch" and a "dash" are when you start cooking, and good cooks who are also good teachers will have you cooking pretty quickly. Good cooks who are not good teachers will just have you mystified. Bad cooks, of course, are another matter altogether.

By the same token, atlases and guidebooks work best when they are used creatively—at least if your point is to get to know a place. You get to know places when you get off the beaten path, even if that means getting lost, slowing down, and wandering around a bit. You are farthest from knowing a place when you confuse the place with the map. If you've ever traveled with someone who spends all their time looking at a map or reading a guidebook, you'll have some sense of what I mean by this. But you may also know people who can carry on wonderful conversations about places they have never been. I think of Emily Dickinson sitting at home in Amherst, Massachusetts, and writing "America" more vibrantly than anyone else in the nineteenth century. It is telling that some of her closest rivals as nineteenth-century writers of America were also homebodies. Walt Whitman traveled, but he often wrote of a West he had barely visited, and he often did it by being in Brooklyn. Henry David Thoreau famously advised against traveling around the world just to count the cats in Zanzibar. Though I highly recommend counting cats wherever you go, I mention this here as a reminder that we make places at least in part by means of what happens between us, which makes "us" and "between" as important as anything in getting to know a place. To carry the cat metaphor one step further, it is more important that the cats (and all the other inhabitants) count in the places you travel than that you count them. As Salman Rushdie has pointed out, you won't find Terry Gilliam's Brazil by traveling to Rio (though you most certainly could find an equally interesting place in the process).[1] This is to tip my hand up front. I don't trust knowing that is separated from doing; but I can't imagine a human being that is not doing. Emily Dickinson at home is most definitely doing; Thoreau at Walden traveled farther than many frequent fliers whose itineraries included Zanzibar; and when e. e. cummings wrote "somewhere i have never traveled . . . ," he took us right to his lover's eyes.[2]

If this invitation works, you will be cooking shortly—and you will probably be lost. If that happens, don't panic. Keep cooking, and be aware that your wandering is acquainting you with a "place" called "philosophy" to the extent that the wandering is part of a "practice" of philosophy. You—we—are making it up as we go along. You can look at the map while you wander, and you can consult a variety of recipes as often as you like. But remember that the map and the recipes will also be available when you find your way home, and that reading them there may help you understand where you've been at the same time that it helps you see "home" in entirely new ways.

Every history contains—at least implicitly—a philosophical argument. This is true also of histories of philosophy and histories of ideas, in which the argument is most often made through subtle decisions about who speaks, who doesn't; who gets the first word, who gets the last;

1. Rushdie, "Location of Brazil," 118–25.
2. Rich, "Vesuvius at Home." cummings, "somewhere i have never travelled."

whose statements are challenged, whose unchallenged. Histories of ideas in particular are most often extended conversations—even if this is not made explicit (and even if it is intentionally suppressed, as in "objective" histories in which the narrator speaks with a godvoice and makes a show of standing nowhere). Every history of ideas also includes (as part of its philosophy) a theory of ideas that, at the very least, takes a position on the relationship between ideas and matter: histories of ideas concern themselves not only with what matters (reflected in choices about order, inclusion, exclusion, and silences) but also with what matter is and how it is (or is not) connected with the ideas that the histories purport to be about. In the broadest sense, this often involves standing on one side or the other of an old argument between materialism and idealism: which comes first—the physical world or ideas? Answers to this question have taken many forms, but it is interesting that they often agree on the necessary interconnection between the two. A history of ideas has to attend to the physical world if for no other reason than that history as an account— spoken, sung, written—requires matter, some medium to carry and some means to receive words; and that an account of the physical world requires ideas, concepts—minimally, words—that can carry meaning. We could choose not to speak at all (and there is some precedent for advocating just this in the way the *Daodejing* begins, for example, and, in the Western tradition, in apophatic theology)—but once we have begun, we have, for better or worse, entered a world in which ideas and things are thoroughly intermingled. Histories of ideas, then, are material histories that attend to (and participate in) the evolution of the physical world and to social/ cultural structures that contribute to it. One might well argue that history of ideas is intrinsically human (at least as long as humans are doing it, and—so far at least—we don't have access to non-human accounts) and that this directs our attention particularly to the human presence in the world and the shape(s) it takes. Humans, more than most inhabitants of this planet, are inclined to alter the shapes of the places in which we live. Those alterations have an impact on our ideas—and they are themselves shaped by the ideas. Think of the architects who designed cities like Shenzhen or Chicago. Structures they imagined have been brought into being by engineers and construction workers, and those structures have a profound impact on how we live and think—sometimes down to the level of who we see, who we don't; who we hear, who we don't; whose voice has authority, whose doesn't . . .

Now, a history of "Western" ideas has the added difficulty of dealing with this term "Western." It is wise to limit the scope of a history, and that is often done by confining it to a particular place and/or time—a history of the T'ang Dynasty or a history of Reconstruction in the United States. Qualifying ideas as "Western" creates the illusion of doing this, but, really, it poses a philosophical and ideological problem disguised as a geographical solution. "Western," we have to ask, vis-à-vis what? Living, as we do, on a globe, terms like "east" and "west" don't mean much when they are isolated. If China, for example, is "East" (Orient) and the United States "West" (Occident), why do I travel west to get from Chicago to Shenzhen? On a globe, everything is west (and east) of everything else (unless it is due north or due south). Even if we grant some meaning to the terms (which do carry spatial significance if we orient ourselves—that is, designate something as "east"—and flatten the globe into a map), they are context sensitive. Vis-à-vis China (if China is east), India is west, though people in the United States often have India in mind when we speak of "Eastern" thought. This is an instance, I will suggest, in which context-sensitivity and a change of physical perspective can provide some philosophical insight. When "Western" is used to modify "ideas," it most often means European or, more broadly, Euro-American. Western thought, then, would be European thought—and in the twentieth century, the center of gravity of that thought, arguably, shifted to the United States. This has little to do with the quality of thought in the United States or elsewhere in the West. It has much to do with ideologically powerful assumptions such as the often repeated and usually unchallenged assertion that the World Trade Center towers on Manhattan destroyed on September 11, 2001, were at the center of the world. This is a mythic statement, structurally equivalent to assertions of world centers in cultures and traditions that "the West" has often labeled "primitive," prerational but establishing the framework within which the exercise of "reason" takes place. It generally goes without saying today that Western culture is "American" culture. A history of "Western" thought, then, could work its way back from a present in which "American" culture is dominant to tease out the origins of that culture: what is the history of "America" and of "Europe"? This is not incompatible with what I said a moment ago about India. Grouping India with the "West" could provide an interesting basis on which to trace an Indo-European category with important distinctions, say, from China. But it is important to bear in mind that what we are talking about here is categories—social constructs that we can play against one another as we seek to "make sense" of the world. Some people would say that this has taken us into the area of genealogy rather than history, but let's not quibble about that right now. I am going to argue that the key to these questions lies in the stories we tell, who tells them, and who we tell them to. Bear in mind that this requires definition (and redefinition) of who "we" are, which also defines—without necessarily intending to—who "they" are. When I ask what stories we tell and who we tell them to, I am aware that we may tell different stories (or tell stories differently) to insiders and outsiders. One of the things we will find ourselves looking for as we try to understand cultures and ideas is foundation myths and stories of origin. Consider this example.

> Once upon a time all the world spoke a single language and used the same words. As men journeyed in the east, they came upon a plain in the land of Shinar and settled there. They said to one another, "Come, let us make bricks and bake them hard"; they used bricks for stone and bitumen for mortar. "Come," they said, "let us build ourselves a city and a tower with its top in the heavens, and make a name for ourselves; or we shall be dispersed all over the earth." Then the Lord came down to see the city and tower which mortal men had built, and he said, "Here they are, one people with a single language, and now they have started to do this; henceforward nothing they have a mind to do will be beyond their reach. Come, let us go down there and confuse their speech, so that they will not understand what they say to one another." So the Lord dispersed them from there all over the earth, and they left off building the city. That is why it is called Babel [Babylon], because the Lord there made a babble of the language of all the world; from that place the Lord scattered men all over the face of the earth. (Gen 11:1–9, NEB)

It might be interesting to try to ascertain when this story was first written down and where—and there are scholars who devote considerable time and energy to doing so—but that is tangential to what I want to do with the story. As it has come to us, it is embedded in a text considered sacred by three major religious traditions. In the earliest form available to us, it is written in Hebrew (though it has been translated into virtually every human language), and it is included in a text that is largely concerned with origins—an extended origin/foundation myth. We'll return to other parts of the myth later. This bit of the myth reads like an answer to a question posed by the world of those who composed it (which is fairly typical of myths). Confronted by a world in which communication is often difficult if not impossible, this myth gives an account (a theory of sorts) of why. On the face of it, as theories go, it's not a very good one, because it can't be tested: the account suggests that we speak different languages (and therefore have trouble communicating) because when we all spoke the same language we were so powerful that we offended (or frightened?) the gods. We can't test it, because we have no way of knowing what would offend the gods (or whether there are indeed gods to be offended). But, on reflection, we may have gotten off on the wrong foot with this reading. For the people who composed this myth, the gods are not a question (though their number might be). The question is language and its relationship to power—and this "answer" is packed with testable (or at least arguable) possibilities. One involves a utilitarian understanding of language. If we ask what language is for, this story answers that it is a tool to help us get things done. In this case, mastery of language is directly related to the height of the tower. We can't build these Shenzhen, Hong Kong, or Chicago skyscrapers if we can't communicate. And there don't seem to be any poets in this crowd who put down their tools and marvel at the beauty of the sounds when all these new languages appear out of nowhere. A second possibility involves an understanding of language and community or cooperation. As it comes to us, the story says the Lord dispersed the people who therefore left off building what has turned from a tower to a city. But in traditional readings of the story, all these folks who were getting along just fine suddenly begin bickering and backbiting when their language changes. They disperse themselves. There's no obvious reason why this should be the case, though, is there? The tower is half built, so the folks building it obviously know what they're doing. Why couldn't they just go on doing it without saying a word? I remember watching my father and my grandfather lay brick (sometimes) without a word between them—and it's not hard to think of skilled activities carried out without spoken language. If you're building something, showing is usually more important than telling in any case. But the story suggests that our human conflicts are somehow related to the confusion (the babel) of our language. That's an interesting possibility. When my grandfather and father were laying brick in silence, they were still communicating. Had they been confused, they wouldn't have worked so well together. A third possibility is a claim about a particular language. This story is written in Hebrew, so the question it asks is not exactly why people speak different languages. It is why "other" people don't speak "our" language. The implicit claim is that Hebrew is the original language and that others are corruptions or derivatives. Similar claims have been made for other languages—Sanskrit, Hanyu, Greek, Arabic. The claim is an instance of mapping the world at the simplest level by imposing a single boundary (the sort of arbitrary line, by the way, that gives spatial significance to terms like "east" and "west").

In the next two chapters, I turn to schematic presentations of two cases that map the world by constructing "the West." First is Christianity understood as a "political" settlement effected by reconstructing a past and transforming the world in its image. Second is philosophy understood as an intellectual achievement of Greek thought foundational to a "West" understood as European.

2

Unsettling Politics

THAT Christianity settled gradually and deliberately into Europe over a period of more than a thousand years is overlooked with surprising regularity in popular accounts of its origins—particularly in popular accounts current among Christians anxious to connect their practice with the practice of a primitive church or an original Christian community. But Christianity is a political settlement, the product of a campaign. More precisely, Christianities are political settlements, products of multiple campaigns in a variety of times and places. To separate product from process, settlement from settling, is to risk serious misunderstanding. In the case of a settlement with the enormous historical and contemporary influence of Christianity, such misunderstanding can have far-reaching political consequences with philosophical implications beyond the boundaries of particular religious communities.

The submersion of settlement in popular accounts of origins is itself an important part of settling, integral to the creation of political bodies, which are often entangled with autochthonous assumptions that are sometimes voiced in autochthonous myths, particularly when they make universal claims or claims about what it means to be human. The first thousand years of Christianity, until roughly 1400 CE, are not only coterminous with its settlement of Europe but also with the emergence of Europe itself. Europe as place is born in Christianity. Christianity as settlement takes place in Europe. This beginning may prove helpful in clarifying and criticizing what happens after 1400 as Europe encounters and, with increasing regularity, *takes* other places. Both the encounter and the taking are connected with struggles articulated in terms of the embodiment, first, of Christianity and, second, of Christians.

In the first thousand years of Christianity, this is evident in the emergence of a canon of Scripture out of an internal struggle with Gnosticism;[1] the emergence of a standard creed out of an internal struggle with Arianism;[2] the emergence of a Christian identity simultaneous with the identification of "other" in a military campaign on two fronts, a (mostly) northern front in confrontation with "pagans" and a (mostly) southern front in confrontation with Muslims; and the struggle to make universal political claims in particular political places.[3] The ease with which early Crusaders could displace their campaign against "Muslim" adversaries into an attack on "Christian" Constantinople is evidence of a third, eastern front in the military campaign, connected with a struggle that begins early over whether Christianity would be Greek or Latin. This eastern front may be understood in part as a struggle between two "universal" languages, and in that regard it is significant that Russian increasingly took the place of Greek as the Greek-speaking remnant of the Roman Empire was conquered by Islam. It is also significant that these "universal" languages were constantly in tension with "local" languages wherever they were adopted or imposed. A fourth front, then, is geographically local: every particular assertion of place is in tension with any settlement that makes universal claims. This becomes increasingly important in European Christianity after 1400, as evidenced in struggles over use of vernacular language in the mass and in translation of Scripture. The simultaneously geographic and military definition of the place of settlement becomes increasingly important at roughly the same time, as evidenced in growing Christian anti-Judaism.[4] For a Christianity and a Europe that increasingly identifies itself militarily in confrontation with an "other," the diasporic Jewish community becomes increasingly an accessible representative of that "other."

1. Lüdemann, *Heretics.*
2. Rubenstein, *When Jesus Became God.*
3. Fletcher, *Barbarian Conversion.* Hopkins, *World Full of Gods.*
4. Cohn-Sherbock, *Crucified Jew.* Crossan, *Who Killed Jesus?*

In this sense, the Jewish diaspora is a prototype for other diasporic communities in unsettling times like the present, characterized by massive displacement of peoples, as surely as Christianity is a prototype for the unsettling character of settling (in Mark Taylor's apt phrase).[5]

Only gradually have popular Christian audiences joined the scholarly consensus that Jesus was Jewish, not Christian—and many audiences have joined that consensus only to the extent that there is no audible collective gasp when the observation is made publicly before a predominantly Christian audience. That something so historically well attested should become consensus only after significant and prolonged struggle is a legacy of the unsettling power of settling and its associated narratives. It is important here because it pushes the foundation of Christianity into at least the second half of the first century. Scholarly examination of historical evidence increasingly pushes that founding further, to the point that it has become more common to maintain that Paul, too, was Jewish to the end.[6] Neither Jesus nor Paul was Christianity's founder, and it makes no sense to speak of Christianity in either of their lifetimes. This has obvious significance for reading the material later incorporated into the New Testament, but it is also significant for understanding Christianity as a political settlement effected over an extended period of time and extended over an expanding space.[7]

It is most sensible to speak of a foundation extended over a period that begins sometime after Paul's death and continues beyond the appropriation of the cross by the Roman army as a martial symbol. That appropriation, in fact, is an integral part of the founding. Rather than speaking of a Christianization of Rome (or a Romanization of Christianity), it is more accurate to speak of a birth of Christianity in a rebirth of Rome that begins in earnest with Constantine, is sharpened theologically by Augustine, and effected politically in the emergence of both the medieval Papacy and (yet another) reconception of Rome in the Carolingian dynasty and the Holy Roman Empire.

The formation of a canon that precedes Constantine's appropriation of the cross takes place in the context of a battle that hinges on the relationship between God and the physical world within which human beings

---

5. Taylor, "Unsettling Issues."

6. Gager, *Reinventing Paul.*

7. Fredriksen, *From Jesus to Christ.* Kee, *Who Are the People of God?*

live. It is significant that this battle takes the form of a struggle for possession of Paul and his thought. When Gnostic teachers, notably Marcion,
claim him, those who would later be known as "orthodox" (because they
won) quickly construct a counter-claim. Marcion's claim separates Paul
sharply from his Jewish roots and takes up the arguably antinomian por-
tions of his writing as a basis upon which to reject Torah and, with it, a
"Testament" identified as "Old." At the same time, Marcion repudiates the
physical world as a symptom of fallenness and labels the creator of that
world an instrument of the fall. Because the "orthodox" counter-claim
does not fully repudiate either of Marcion's separations, his conceptualization of a "New" Testament that supersedes an "Old" one gains a foothold,
as does his conceptualization of a physical world that is essentially evil.

Narratives that become the foundation myths of Christianity, then,
are forged at least partly at the point of a separation from Judaism and
a separation from the physical world. They are adopted into a Roman
Empire that is increasingly concerned with maintaining boundaries that
separate Roman civilization from an uncultivated, uncivilized (and hence
"pagan") north. Rome already had a venerable tradition of incorporating
newcomers by "civilizing" them—a symbolic, linguistic, and ritual practice
of bringing them into the city (sometimes by bringing the city to them).
This tradition continues as Christianity emerges. As Fletcher and others
have noted, though Christian elements creep beyond Roman boundaries
into Gothic culture, the Goths resist its spread at exactly those moments
where central features of Gothic culture appear to be threatened.

A reading of Augustine's polemical writing makes it clear that this
resistance was also present in Rome. One rationale for Augustine's *City of
God* is repudiation of the claim that Rome's decay begins with its adoption
of Christianity and abandonment of ancestral gods. Gothic and Roman
objections are ultimately engulfed by a rising tide of Christianity that is
itself a redefinition of Rome. What began as a struggle between the Goths
and Rome is transformed into a struggle for control of Roman identity.
This is also relevant to the East-West divide referenced earlier, a struggle
that is more or less contemporary with the encounter between Romans and
Goths. Along the East-West dimension, the question is initially whether
Rome would be Greek or Latin. Along the North-South dimension, the
question is initially whether it would be Gothic.

Theologically, both questions revolve around the Arian controversy
and just how relationships both within God (as Trinitarian doctrine be-

gins to emerge) and between God and humankind are to be understood, particularly as Christology and pneumatology are worked out, theologically and devotionally.[8] Linguistically, they revolve around a struggle for universality that asks both whether Rome is to speak Latin or Greek and just how "universal" languages (such as Latin and Greek) relate to "local" ones. Both questions, of course, are cultural as well as linguistic. To ask how universal languages relate to local ones is to pose a central problem for the struggle that erupts into violence and schism at the time of the Protestant Reformations. Political dimensions are evident in divergent forms of centralization practiced by the Byzantine and Western Empires and in decentralized political practices that characterized many of the peoples of Europe who took on Roman and therefore Christian identity as that identity was established northward. Christian identity is intimately connected in this process with repudiation of a former identity, in much the same way as the incorporation into Rome was associated with repudiation of former identities. Adopt the language, adopt the culture, cease to be "barbarian," and become "civilized."

It is not until late in the second and early in the third century with Tertullian (150–222) that Latin is employed in writing that would become ecclesiastically and theologically influential.[9] This does not mark the beginning of the struggle between Greek and Latin so much as it signals that the struggle has developed to a point at which a Christian identity simultaneously separated from Greek language and from Judaism can be expressed confidently in Latin—even though the narratives to which the emerging community looks for its foundation myths are written in Greek and Hebrew. There is precedent for this development in Virgil's appropriation of Greek narrative for his great Roman foundation myth, the *Aeneid*. That this myth was so readily Christianized by later generations is significant, particularly since the founding of Rome in Virgil's account is coterminous with the murder of Turnus, who represents the indigenous people of Italy. And that Tertullian is representative of this development is instructive, given the extent to which the subsequent split is as much a separation from Plato and Neoplatonic Greek philosophy as it is a separation from the Greek language. Though Tertullian's orthodoxy was called into question, his depiction of reason and faith as antithetical has been enormously

8. Rubenstein, *When Jesus Became God.*
9. Fletcher, *Barbarian Conversion.*

influential. Greek writers, including Clement (150–215) and Origen (182–254), are identified with Neoplatonic thought, while Latin writers increasingly take a different tack in their development of Christianity. In Tertullian, the split is a repudiation of reason, but in the Latin church it is more explicitly a redefinition of reason that, in Scholasticism, will be connected not with Plato but with Aristotle—an Aristotle that is as Latin as the Vulgate, about which I will have more to say in a moment.

Carolyn Walker Bynum connects this linguistic, social, and political development with the development in Christianity, from the beginning of the third century to the middle of the fourteenth, of a conception of human identity as psychosomatic unity. She notes the persistence of "concern for material and structural continuity" over these eleven centuries:

> The idea of person, bequeathed by the Middle Ages to the modern world, was not a concept of soul escaping body or soul using body; it was a concept of self in which physicality was integrally bound to sensation, emotion, reasoning, identity—and therefore finally to whatever one means by salvation. Despite its suspicion of flesh and lust, Western Christianity did not hate or discount the body. Indeed, person was not person without body, and body was the carrier or the expression (although the two are not the same thing) of what we today call individuality.[10]

At the same time that this conception of an individual as psychosomatic unity is developing, a body politic is developing that will provide the context in later centuries for assertion of individual rights. Development of that body politic is as concerned with material and structural continuity—in the form of a church and of an empire—as is development of an idea of person understood as psychosomatic unity. Unity of person is not only psychosomatic but also sociopolitical (a concept that includes the ecclesiastical). In the European settlement of Christianity, the body and the body politic develop hand-in-hand.

One of the more striking narratives from the beginning of this development is the account of the execution of a young Roman woman named Perpetua early in the third century at Carthage in North Africa.[11] Like other martyrs of the time, Perpetua understands her Christian identity as requiring her to repudiate both her body and her Roman identity. This repudiation means rejection of her family (including an infant who is still

10. Bynum, *Resurrection of the Body in Western Christianity*, 11.
11. Salisbury, *Perpetua's Passion*.

nursing) and willing, strikingly heroic, submission to death. It is ironic that heroic displays such as that of Perpetua, and the mythologized accounts of those displays, tilted the development of Christianity toward the center of Roman life. Though Roman authorities plausibly expected such publicly visible deaths to serve as deterrents to participation in a growing movement, they appear instead to have inspired participation. Growing participation made the Roman deterrence strategy increasingly costly, until it was finally abandoned. At the point of its abandonment, an identification that had required a double death—figuratively, in renunciation of Roman identity and, literally, in submission to martyrdom— was transformed into an identification that was indistinguishable from Roman identity. To be a Christian, increasingly, was to live as a citizen of Rome—virtually the opposite of what it meant for Perpetua.

Fletcher locates the beginning of rural mission in the last half of the third century, with Gregory Thaumaturgis (210–270), a student of Origen who is also said to have experienced the earliest recorded vision of the Blessed Virgin in Christian history.[12] The Virgin Mary plays an increasingly important role in popular devotion and conversion of "pagan" folk who live outside the city limits.[13]

At roughly the same time that rural "mission" is developing, Christianity is moving toward the center of Roman life. The Roman settlement of Christianity moves simultaneously toward the center and toward the periphery. Significantly, movement toward the periphery does not marginalize Christianity or render it peripheral so much as it incorporates the periphery into the center. In this regard, Christianity succeeds in much the same way that Rome had succeeded before it. This is reflected in devotion to the cross that flourishes from the beginning of the fourth century, when Constantine's mother, Empress Helena, discovers the "True Cross." From this moment, the cross, which had been rare, becomes "a frequent motif in Christian art—for example, on gravestones."[14] It would be hard to find a symbol closer to the center than the Emperor's mother, and so Helena's identification with the cross is as significant as its later adoption by Constantine. That such a central figure would turn backward to seek and embrace such a symbol of marginality is significant for the development of

---

12. Fletcher, *Barbarian Conversion*, 34.

13. Cunneen, *In Search of Mary*.

14. Fletcher, *Barbarian Conversion*, 56.

Christianity. It would be difficult to script a more stunning representation of the incorporation of the periphery into the center than the Emperor coming to the cross by way of his mother! The embrace is initiated in the granting of tolerance to Christians by Emperor Galerius (311), but it is solidified in Constantine's Edict of Milan (313), which declared toleration of Christians "perpetual," and the exemption of Christian clergy from taxation (319). Note that Christianity is not simply and suddenly adopted by Constantine; it is gradually established as it works its way toward the center of Roman society.

At the same time that it is working its way toward the center of Roman society, Christianity is systematized at the Council of Nicaea (325). Paradoxically, that systematization provides the catalyst for separation between Greek and Latin churches at almost the same time that the Byzantine Empire (which lasts from 330 until 1453) comes into being. Again, linguistic divisions couple with theological arguments as well as political and cultural divisions to effect the subsequent European settlement of Christianity.

That the strategy of that settlement parallels the destiny Virgil narrated in his *Aeneid* is evident in figures such as Martin of Tours (336–397). Born in what is now Hungary, Martin served as Bishop of Tours from 371 to 397.[15] Commenting on the violence of Martin's mission, Fletcher writes "Miracles, wonders, exorcisms, temple-torching and shrine smashing were in themselves acts of evangelization."[16] Sulpicius writes that Martin built a church or monastery wherever he destroyed a pagan shrine. Pagan shrines are regularly appropriated, as are pagan celebrations. Witness the fact that, by 336, the birth of Christ is celebrated on Saturnalia (December 25) in Rome. The Vulgate, the Latin translation of the Bible by Jerome (340–420) that would become normative for the Western Church, is an integral part of this strategy of appropriation.

Fletcher associates the decline of Roman power in the fifth century with the increasing power of bishops, who stepped in to fill gaps in administration. He refers to an "upward drift in the public profile of the bishop"[17] and points to unique dimensions of Irish Christianity that would become significant for Christianity's European settlement. In the first place,

15. Ibid., 40ff.
16. Ibid., 45.
17. Ibid., 51.

Patrick appears to have been (during the fifth century) the "first person in Christian history to take the scriptural injunctions literally; to grasp that teaching all nations meant teaching even barbarians who lived beyond the frontiers of the Roman empire."[18] Beyond the obvious significance for the spread of Christianity, this shift to conversion of "barbarians" also marks the moment at which Christianity adopts the uniquely Roman tactic of expansion by civilization. Because it begins in Ireland, it is significant that "the fundamental political unit" in Ireland was the *tuath*, which Fletcher describes as "a human grouping held together partly by kinship, partly by clientage, in occupation of a shifting zone of territory under the presidency of a dynasty of kings maintained by tribute in kind." *Tuatha* were not geographically defined, and Fletcher describes them using a biological metaphor: "Like biological cells, *tuatha* were constantly on the move, splitting, fusing, splitting again, as one king achieved a temporary supremacy over his neighbors only to lose it after a few years."[19]

Because this Irish "city" is not strictly located or locatable geographically, it possesses a flexibility and mobility that would not be available to more rigid political models. The Irish monks responsible for carrying Roman Christianity into continental Europe adopted a model akin to the *tuath* and thus created a variant of Roman Christianity that existed in tension with Roman political organization in Europe. Fletcher contrasts the structure of monasticism (which is primarily Celtic) with "Roman" ecclesiastical structure and asserts that monastic structure was more adaptable, particularly to the fluid "political" structure of Ireland.[20] Note that there is a tension between an emerging ecclesiastical structure built around bishops who adopt a Roman administrative model and an intermittently active civil authority built around a similar model but with different personnel— as well as tension between a monastic and an episcopal ecclesiastical structure. Each claims to be Roman, and each claims to be Christian. As Fletcher notes, there are also layers of tension that include "the world of rural pagans slowly being coaxed into some semblance of Christian belief and observance by activists like Martin of Tours, alongside the Catholic bishops in their cities, the Catholic suburban monasteries, the Catholic gentry and the Catholic middle class" as well as "an Arian clerical hierar-

18. Ibid., 86.
19. Ibid., 89.
20. Ibid., 90–91.

chy, Arian kings and queens and warrior aristocrats, Arian churches with Arian liturgies being sung within them. This religious apartheid persisted in the kingdoms concerned until their governing circles decided to go over to Catholicism" in the sixth century.[21]

Benedict (480–547), the author of the rule that—in one form or another—comes to govern virtually all of Western monasticism, is a figure of this century, as is Clovis, whose conversion in 496 brings the Franks into Christendom. Between them, they cover military strategies for the expansion of Christianity (after the conversion of Clovis, that expansion is increasingly indistinguishable from the expansion of the Frankish kingdom) as well as the classic technique of rural evangelization that transfers ritual from one religious loyalty to another.[22] Fletcher cites the shrine of Hilary of Poitiers at Javols as an example. Both strategies risk a thin conversion in which a veneer of Christianity (or Roman civilization, or identification with the Kingdom of the Franks) is spread over a "pagan" base. Survival of pre-Christian symbols and religious practice in areas long Christianized may be evidence of such a thin conversion. Fletcher speaks of an evangelizing campaign that John of Ephesus undertook in the middle of the sixth century in what is now western Turkey:

> In the course of several years' work, he and his helpers demolished temples and shrines, felled sacred trees, baptized 80,000 persons, built ninety-eight churches and founded twelve monasteries. And this was in the heart of the empire, an area where there had been a Christian presence since the time of St. Paul, not in some out-of-the-way corner like Cornwall or Galicia. In 598 Pope Gregory wrote to the bishop of Terracina to express dismay at a report that had reached him to the effect that the inhabitants of those parts were worshiping sacred trees. Again, not a remote spot; Terracina is on the coast between Rome and Naples, its countryside traversed by the Via Appia, one of the busiest highways of the Mediterranean world.[23]

Frank notes that "Becoming Christian always also meant being incorporated into the Frankish empire. Missions were planned and churches and monasteries founded under the protection of the Frankish kings and served to enlarge their realm. The other side of this missionary policy was

21. Ibid., 99.
22. Ibid., 49.
23. Ibid., 62–63.

a politically motivated resistance to the acceptance of Christianity. This resistance was crushed by force."[24] He emphasizes the political character of Christianity's European settlement:

> the mass was not a liturgical proclamation which also served the edification of the community, but a cultic event which communicated grace objectively. The focus was on the presence of Christ, often in a physical and reified permanent form. Everything depended on the transformation of bread and wine, and all else in the mass was an extra. People saw the presence of "sanctifying grace" through the transformation in the mass. So the mass had to be celebrated as often as possible (frequent and daily mass). The mass was celebrated for the people, but not with the people. For this reason the adoption of Latin and alien cultic language was not a problem. The important thing was not understanding the cult, but its correct performance by the priest.[25]

Frank associates the decline of the city with the rise of feudalism, both with occupation of Roman territory by new peoples who had no knowledge of city life and administration. The influx/occupation exacerbated the decline of the city and fed the rise of feudalism. This process is in turn connected with the emergence of "proprietary" churches[26] and the breakup of the "bishop's house" in the eleventh century.[27] The bishop becomes a representative of the king (hence joining the aristocracy); both bishops and monasteries are incorporated into the crown. What is often described as "conversion" of "the barbarians" looks more like incorporation of the church—an alienation of people (bishops, priests, monks) and objects (churches, monasteries) from the church to the crown. He refers to the ruler's "sacral dignity": "Three elements above all supported the sacral notion of the ruler: political religion, the theory of proprietary churches, and the idea of the king." He goes on to say that "we can sum up the content of political religion briefly in the statement: all religion is public and all that is public is religious. For *res publica* and religion belonged together. This unity needs to be emphasized. A division into

---

24. Frank, *Concise History of the Mediaeval Church*, 4.

25. Ibid., 6.

26. Ibid., 21.

27. Ibid., 25.

two fundamentally different (or even only separate) spheres was simply unimaginable."[28]

As Frank describes the process:

> . . . under the domination of the papacy, the emergent West gained a new ecclesiastical ecumenicity which led to the *ecclesia urbis* (=the church of the city, i.e. Rome) becoming the norm for the *ecclesia orbis* (=the church of the globe, i.e. Western Christendom). This development was complex and was carried forward (and also hindered) by a variety of forces. For in the decline of the ancient empire not only the political *ecumene* but also the ecclesiastical *ecumene* had been lost, since the latter had ultimately been based on the institutions of the empire and the emperor. What persisted of the old church ecumenicity in the Western provinces was a provincialized awareness on the part of the episcopal communities that they belonged together. But their synodical life, which initially was still strong, was taken into the service of the new kingdoms. The autonomous ecclesiastical episcopal synods became councils of the realm under royal leadership.[29]

Because Christianity settled into agricultural communities whose "archaic religion" was primarily concerned with the "earthly and heavenly well-being of individual and community," in which "the blessings of the gods carried obligations" that included "observation of the customs and usages handed down from antiquity," it had, by late antiquity, "taken on the features of a religion of cultic observances, involving the precise observance of divine commandments and the careful performance of cultic regulations."[30] After about 500, the political community increasingly absorbed the ecclesiastical—meaning that the political community identified itself more and more with Christianity while the ecclesiastical community took on functions identified as political. As a result, the individual was no longer

> a "citizen" of two "communities," as in Christian antiquity, but merely in the ontological sense a "citizen of two worlds," earth and heaven, this world and the next. On earth there was a political community which in terms of traditional religion understood itself as a sacral alliance that absorbed the church community into itself. This social monism of political religion is to be regarded as

28. Ibid., 48–49.
29. Ibid., 34.
30. Ibid., 12.

the metaphysical basis of the proprietary church system of the early Middle Ages and also the sacral dimension of imperial power.[31]

This will prove particularly important for the Lutheran Reformation and Lutheran political theory. Luther's doctrine of "two kingdoms" is not a separation of Church and State, but a relocation of the sacral dimension of imperial power. It does not posit two human communities or a human community and a divine one, but one God's two rules in a community that, though it may appear divided, is, nevertheless, fundamentally one. Frank describes two theories, which he labels "theocratic monism" and "theocratic dualism," both of which designate the king "as the visible head of the church." The monistic theory explicitly designates the king as ruler, while the dualistic theory does so implicitly, acknowledging the power of the papacy before subordinating it to temporal authority.[32]

That Christianity settled into agricultural communities meant that its expansion was understood as "rural mission," directly addressed in a sixth-century sermon of Martin of Braga, *De Correctione Rusticorum*, cited by Fletcher. Martin, a native of what is now Hungary, was Bishop of Braga (in northern Portugal) by 572. He "begins with a brief sketch of sacred history, firmly locating the pagan god among the demonic ministers of the Devil when he was cast out of heaven."[33] He lists "pagan" rituals and replaces them with Christian ones, prompting Fletcher to comment on the haziness of the line that divides pagan from Christian rituals at this point. What is understood as "rural mission" often simply recasts the Roman strategy of civilization: pagans are brought into the city, and, while the city is transformed as well as the pagans, it maintains its existence and its identity across time. In fact, the recognition that maintaining existence and identity across time depends on transformational processes is a particular genius that Rome bequeathed to Christianity.

Somewhat akin to the internal tension between universal and local language that Christianity took on with its Roman identity is an internal tension between settlement and pilgrimage. Pilgrimage became progressively more important as Christianity settled in Europe, and one form that settlement took is self-identification as a perpetual pilgrim. Amandus (590–675), for example, born into a landed family of Gallo-Roman

31. Ibid., 15.

32. Ibid., 50–52.

33. Ibid., 53.

descent, joined a monastic community, then journeyed to Tours, where he made a vow "that he might never be permitted to return to his own land but might spend his whole life on pilgrimage as an exile for Christ." He later went to Rome, where he experienced a vision of St. Peter, who told him to return to Gaul and take up the task of preaching. After returning, he became a bishop (probably in the late 620s). He later took up missionary work again, attempting (unsuccessfully) to evangelize the Basques, and received a seat for his bishopric (647) at Maastricht.[34] Here the tension is palpable, but it is also critical to an ability to "settle" anywhere precisely by settling nowhere, by remaining perpetually unsettled. An exile for Christ whose whole life is a pilgrimage is equally at home (and equally homeless) no matter where she or he is, and no matter when. Perpetual pilgrimage understood as exile is a strategy by which to transcend place, a strategy that underwrites potentially limitless extension in space.

Christianity's European settlement accelerated beginning late in the sixth century. Augustine of Canterbury departed on his mission to the Anglo-Saxons in 596, and Christianity grew steadily among the Germans and among the Slavs along their borders from the seventh to the ninth century at the same time that church institutions were consolidated.[35] Settlement involved conversion not only of people but also of places and rituals. Fletcher notes that

> Bede warmly commended Pope Boniface IV (608–15) for acquiring the enormous temple in Rome known as the Pantheon and turning it into the Christian church which it still is: Sta Maria Rotonda . . . It neatly exemplifies the tactics approved by Boniface's master Gregory I. This conversion of pagan buildings or cult-sites to Christian uses was happening all over western Europe during our period. Sometimes it is explicitly referred to in our written sources, as in the stories told of Martin of Tours by Sulpicius Severus, or in the biographer's assertion that Boniface used timber from the sacred oak of Geismar to build a Christian chapel. Sometimes the evidence is archaeological . . . Sometimes the evidence comes from place-names.[36]

Fletcher goes on to write that

---

34. Ibid., 147–54.
35. Ibid., 9–10.
36. Fletcher, *Barbarian Conversion*, 254–55.

among the most imposing of the Christian claims was to transcend time and place. Nowhere was this claim more impressive
than at the shrines of the saints. Though dead in the body the saint
was there, living on in the tomb. St. Peter at Rome, St. Martin at
Tours, St. Cuthbert at Lindisfarne, St. Boniface at Fulda, St. James
at Compostela (a new arrival in the ninth century); all these and
numberless others were active, vital forces transmitting waves of
spiritual energy into miracles of help and healing for human suppliants. The power of prayer leapt across human frontiers of the here
and now. Prayer caused Imma's bonds to be loosed. Prayer linked
distantly separated monasteries like Fulda and Montecassino.
Prayer maintained the emotional cohesion of kin and community
across the river of death.[37]

Transcendence of time and space is paradoxically connected with
presence, pilgrimage, and place. Strictly speaking, it is more accurate to
say that Christianity claimed to transcend time and space, not time and
place—and that one of the most important ways it effected this claim was
in its construction of place, in shrines and saints as Fletcher notes, but
also in pilgrimage. Christianity placed persons in journeys conceptual-
ized spatially and temporally. Shrines and saints universalized space by
disconnecting persons from the particular places in which they were
born. Calendars universalized time by disconnecting persons from events
located in their particular places, by connecting them with events that
occurred elsewhere. To transcend time and space, to leap across human
frontiers of the here and now, persons had to come unstuck, as recognized
much later in Kurt Vonnegut's aptly named Billy Pilgrim.[38]

Coming "unstuck," I am convinced, is an appropriate metaphor for
the condition of the local in a globalized socioeconomic system. The metaphor poses a problem, consideration of which I must defer. For now, suffice
it to say that this is where philosophical reconsideration of the "theological" category of "real presence" undertaken in the seventeenth century by
the Cambridge Platonists and Anne Conway and at the end of the seventeenth and beginning of the eighteenth by Gottfried Leibniz is politically
significant today. Christianity as settlement poses a problem that directs
our attention to insights of that theological discussion (to which we will
turn in chapter 6) as aids to local vision in our own globalizing context.

37. Ibid., 258.
38. Vonnegut, *Slaughterhouse-five*.

3

The Virtue of Hesitation

"PHILOSOPHY" is an English transliteration of a Greek word, *philosophia*, derived from *philosophos*, a word used as early as Pythagoras (fl. 531 BCE, over 2500 years ago). Both the practice (*philosophia*) and the one who practices it (*philosophos*) are named by compounds of two words, *phileo* and *sophia* or *sophos*.

Phileo is one of several Greek words for "love." It is sometimes translated as "brotherly" love, but that's a bit misleading. It most often carries a connotation of affection or devotion and conveys a sense of friendship that involves long-term commitment. It is a "passion" as opposed to an "action" in the sense that it is something one undergoes rather than something one does, but it is not a momentary thing. This distinguishes it from *eros*, which is more likely to evoke an image of being swept off one's feet. It is less sharply distinguished from *agape*, though Christian writers (long after Pythagoras) used that term specifically for the "selfless" love of God for humankind. The choice of *phileo* is important because it evokes an image of friendship and devotion over a lifetime rather than a momentary passion. In broad terms, *phileo* is associated with devotion directed toward community; *eros* is associated with desire directed toward possession; and *agape* is associated with self-sacrifice directed toward identity. All three aspects of "love" are important for understanding the "Western" philosophical tradition. Much has been made in the twentieth century of the association of knowledge with desire. Without diminishing the importance of that association, it's worthwhile, I think, to return also to the earlier association of knowledge with devotion and friendship.

Sophia designated both "skill" or "practical knowledge" and "wisdom." Given the later tendency to brand philosophers "impractical," it's important not to overlook this early association with practicality: the *sophoi* (plural of *sophos*) were so named because of their life experience and practical knowledge, not because of some "academic" credentials.[1] Sophia was personified as a woman and associated in Hebrew tradition with the *Shekinah* (God's presence with humankind, also feminine) and in early Christian tradition with the *Logos* (sometimes translated as "word," but also connected with God's presence—as in the prologue to the Gospel of John, "In the beginning was the word, and the word was with God, and the word was God . . .").

Philosophos may have been coined by Pythagoras and his followers as a way to distinguish themselves from the *sophoi*—sages who, in the Greek-speaking world as in many other parts of the world, were sometimes granted a semi-mythic status. For our purposes, it is most important to bear in mind that the name implies a distinction between someone who possesses wisdom and someone who is devoted to it. Pythagoras perhaps thought of himself and his followers as friends of wisdom, its devotees rather than its possessors. Socrates (469–399 BCE) made much of this distinction: the philosopher is one who seeks wisdom as a lifelong friend rather than one who possesses it. For Socrates, in fact, the philosopher is marked by his or her awareness that s/he does not possess wisdom—or possesses it only to the extent that s/he knows that s/he does not know.

That Pythagoras coined the name by which philosophers have been known in "the West" is important for a number of reasons. First, it highlights the extent to which the Greek language formed the concepts and ideas of early Western philosophy. Second, because Pythagoras lived and worked on the Italian peninsula, it highlights the extent to which the Greek speaking world included a cultural and geographical area much larger than what we now know as Greece. This is one indicator of a multicultural matrix for Western philosophy. And third, given Pythagoras's

---

1. In this connection, it's worth noting that *phileo*, applied to an object, could mean "apt" or "inclined toward." The *philosophos*, then, would be one inclined toward skill or practical knowledge.

apparent appropriation of Egyptian ideas, it provides one bridge from the Greek-speaking milieu of early Western philosophy to its African roots—another indicator of its multicultural matrix.

We will return to this concept of a "multicultural matrix" later. First, however, a word about the discipline of philosophy as lifelong devotion to wisdom is in order.

Two concerns appear to have driven philosophy at its origins: a concern with what is and a concern with what works—what we might now call theoretical and practical knowledge. These concerns have stayed with philosophy throughout its history and have surfaced in philosophical speculation across a wide variety of cultural boundaries. We will be especially concerned with variations on the "practical" question when we turn later to pragmatism. That "practical" question probably lies at the root of philosophical speculation as it developed in Egypt and early on in the Greek-speaking world, where it was closely associated with the kind of applied mathematics that led to some of the remarkable architectural achievements of Egypt and the Mediterranean world. It was also associated with the sophisticated observational astronomy (and astrology) of Egypt and Persia (as well as China and, later, the Aztecs and Incas).

Most of the early schools of philosophy that influenced the development of the "Western" philosophical tradition seem to have revolved around a conjunction of the two kinds of questions: what works is inextricably connected with what is, and a "passion" for wisdom involves a passionate investigation of Nature (*physis*). Egyptian schools of philosophy and their Greek offspring concerned themselves with "natural" philosophy and often sought to identify the basic "stuff" (*hylē*) of which the universe is made and the basic "structure" that orders the universe. This sort of philosophical speculation is labeled ontology and is the predecessor of modern physics as well as the still (sometimes) thriving philosophical discipline of ontology.

"Ontology," like "philosophy," is a compound of two Greek words: *ontos* (being) and *logos* (which we've already encountered as "word" but which might better be understood here as language). It is language—disciplined conversation—about "being."

Rather early on, many philosophical schools came to the conclusion that there is a discrepancy between what is and what we as human beings are able to know. This led philosophers such as Socrates to shift their attention from language about being to language about knowing.

Combining the Greek word for knowing (*episteme*) with *logos* gives us the name by which this discipline is known: epistemology.

Socrates is also often associated with another shift of philosophical attention that formulates another kind of question and gives rise to another discipline within philosophy. Not only do we ask what is and what works; we also ask what matters. Our language is not only about being and knowing but also about valuing. This, too, has a name—axiology—formed from two Greek words *axios* (value) and *logos*. This discipline is usually further divided into ethics (concerned with "the good") and aesthetics (concerned with "the beautiful").

Since so much of philosophy, whether written or not, is concerned with communication, it is no surprise that questions about language have also been integral parts of philosophical speculation from the beginning. No matter how we respond to questions about being, knowing, and valuing, the response itself entangles us (even if our response is silence) in language. And so, philosophy has traditionally associated itself with the disciplines of grammar, logic, and rhetoric. How do we communicate truth, and how do we move others in relation to appearance, reality, or both?

Let's stop for a moment and see what we've done so far in this chapter before we turn to more specifically historical background.

Philosophy is a passion for wisdom, a passion most like the devotion one practices toward dear friends and family. It is a long-term commitment directed toward community and communication, specifically toward a community formed around the presence of wisdom in communication: the word becomes flesh and dwells among us . . .

This devotion to wisdom has organized itself around several types of questions—questions that remain important today:

> What is?
>
> What (and how) do we know?
>
> What matters?

These questions are associated with subdisciplines of philosophy:

> Ontology (language about being)
>
> Epistemology (language about knowing)
>
> Axiology (language about valuing)
>
> Ethics (concerned with "the good")

Aesthetics (concerned with "the beautiful")

. . . and disciplines of language and communication sometimes included in philosophy and always associated with it:

Grammar (concerned especially with classification)

Logic (concerned especially with validity)

Rhetoric (concerned especially with persuasion)

That gives us a rather broad range of disciplines with which to be concerned—but it also assures us that we do not have to be "in control" of the methods or content of these disciplines in order to practice philosophy. That is both a more modest and a more long-term task, a task that some of you will find maddening (because it will not come to an end), others of you will find delightful (because it will not come to an end), and some of you—I hope—will find both. To be a philosopher is to be a devoted friend of wisdom. The practice of that devotion has been associated in many cultures with a kind of divine madness.

I should warn you that some cultures are more tolerant of such madness than is "Western" culture—but that makes it all the more important in "Western" culture. As Emily Dickinson (who was indisputably a dear friend of wisdom) wisely put it: "A little Madness in the Spring/ Is wholesome even for the King,/ But God be with the Clown—/ Who ponders this tremendous scene—/ This whole Experiment of Green/ As if it were his own!"[2]

Paulin Hountondji argues that philosophy is not a system but a history, by which he means that it is open-ended and in process rather than closed and complete. He also argues for a "dialectical" understanding of the development and makes specific proposals regarding African philosophy. Whether you are interested in African philosophy or not, the specific proposals are relevant to the extent that they suggest ways in which "local" philosophies might develop within the "global" process (or history) of philosophy itself. Hountondji pictures it as a "debate" (some philosophers have preferred to call it a "conversation") in which everyone who does philosophy is involved, from generation to generation. This concept suggests that philosophy is not a "system" in the sense of a complete truth or set of truths, and it suggests that there is no absolutely true "system" in this sense. The "truth" of philosophy lies in what Hountondji calls "the relative

2. Poem #1333 in *Poems of Emily Dickinson*.

of an infinite, open-ended process . . . Truth cannot be a set of definite, untranscendable propositions but rather the process by which we look for propositions more adequate than others. In a way, then, truth is the very act of looking for truth, of enunciating propositions and trying to justify and found them."[3]

It's worth noting, I think, how similar this is to the idea (introduced in the previous chapter) of "the word" dwelling among us. The lifelong friend of wisdom lives in such a way as to embody wisdom, effectively collapsing the distinction between the seeking and that which is sought. Since we invoked Pythagoras in the process of developing that idea, we might also bear in mind that many schools of philosophy, including the one with which he was associated, have insisted that philosophy is a way of life, as in A. J. Muste's claim that "There is no way to peace . . . Peace is the way . . ."

Hountondji argues that the dream of "wholeness" that he identifies especially with Hegel and Spinoza is both necessary and vain. It is necessary, he says, because "Every one of us likes to think that we pronounce the truth as a court of law pronounces a judgment. We cannot persist in our thought without this belief. The truth of our discourse, like truth in general, is not only an ideological myth but also a necessary and productive ideological myth." It is vain, he says simply, because "history cannot be stopped . . . it cannot be neutralized, and its surprises cannot be reduced."[4]

Hountondji's discussion of "African philosophy" is itself a contribution to the definition of philosophy. After that discussion has gone on for several pages, he says that "we are now at the heart of the matter. An individual act of discourse is not yet a philosophy. Individual discourse (as opposed to silent group discourse), the discursive intervention (as opposed to passive acquiescence) are no doubt necessary conditions; but they cannot in themselves create the act of philosophizing. On the social level the last proposition means this: granted that philosophy can exist historically only through a literature, that it is properly speaking a special kind of literature, it does not follow that all literature is philosophical."[5]

---

3. Hountondji, *African Philosophy*, 72–73

4. Ibid., 74.

5. Ibid., 81.

Hountondji (like anyone else who does a history of philosophy) is concerned to make distinctions, to select some things for inclusion and others for exclusion: so he distinguishes philosophy from mythology, from poetry, and from ordinary discourse: "Every thinker," he writes, "is not a philosopher. This point must be made clearly so that we can rid ourselves of the common illusion once and for all." In responding to the "trick" question "what is philosophy?" he offers more distinctions (even though he refuses to answer at this point): philosophy is distinguished from poetry, from narrative, from myth, from proverb, from aphorism, from history, and from biography.[6] He makes a broad distinction between "artistic" and "scientific" literature (remember this later), and assigns philosophy to the latter category: it is "scientific" rather than "artistic." "Roughly speaking," he writes,

> one can say that a poem or a novel is valuable in itself; it is inde-
> pendent of the general history of poetry or the novel. A philo-
> sophical or mathematical work, on the other hand, is intelligible
> only as a moment in a debate that sustains and transcends it. It
> always refers to antecedent positions, either to refute them or to
> confirm and enrich them. It takes on meaning only in relation to
> that history, in relation to the terms of an ever-changing debate
> in which the sole stable element is the constant reference to one
> self-same object, to one sphere of experience, the characteriza-
> tion of which, incidentally, is itself part of the evolution. Scientific
> literature, in short, is thoroughly historical.[7]

Broadly speaking, Hountondji argues that scientific literature is historical, artistic literature ahistorical: "In the strictest sense of the term, art
has no history, although it unfolds in history. Philosophy, on the other
hand, like any other science, is historical in its very substance. It has the
intrinsic historicity of a pluralistic discourse, in which different interlocu-
tors question and answer one another within a generation or from one
generation to another."[8]

Hountondji wants to maintain that philosophy is history itself: it is a
productive process, a "second-order history borne by empirical history."
He describes Kant as seeing philosophy as the story of the failures of human attempts to grapple with transcendental problems. "The structure

6. Ibid., 83.
7. Ibid.
8. Ibid.

of the history of philosophy is similar to that attributed by Bachelard to science: 'What happens is not a development from old doctrines to the new; but rather an envelopment of old thoughts by the new.'"[9]

Hountondji's own argument illustrates a discovery that has been influential in some strands of both philosophy and theology: it is often more useful to proceed by saying what a thing is not (by negation) than by attempting to say what it is (by affirmation).

V. Y. Mudimbe takes this up by examining the limit between what is and what is not said, and this leads him to investigate three "categories" employed by Herodotus (ca. 484–425 BCE) and others to separate the world into "us" and "them" (speaking loosely, of course—to Herodotus all of "us" who do not speak Greek would be "them").

Notice that when Mudimbe points out that Pliny's (23–79 CE) map "proceeds eastward" while Herodotus's map "goes westward," he is pointing out more generally the tendency of our maps to proceed outward from ourselves or from what we take to be "civilized": the movement is from civilization to its opposite. The distinction between "marked" and "unmarked" is another way of putting this: what is "central" is also "normal" and therefore does not require explanation.[10] What is "peripheral" is "exotic" and therefore does. Mudimbe notes that maps are "scientific" projects and that they "totalize" knowledge.

As I said, Mudimbe explores three "categories" employed by Herodotus: *barbaroi* (foreigners), *agrioi* (savages), and *oiorpata* (women who kill men). He uses the exploration to suggest that "a place" becomes a "reference-schema which haunts a tradition and its knowledge." Space becomes "a general organizing principle of knowledge and cultures . . . Triumph of the *politikon* and the *politeia* i[s] a conquering cultural act of conversion: Yet does it not really express simply the fear of *agrioi*, *oiorpata*, and other monsters that is the fear of difference?" Fear of difference is an important factor in the development of Western thought, and it is often manifested in containment strategies that involve origin accounts. I will return to this in a moment when I discuss Martin Bernal's *Black Athena*. Before turning to containment strategies, though, an outline of the African background of Greek philosophy will be helpful due to the central role played (as Mudimbe notes) by the invention of Africa in that tradition and because

9. Ibid., 90.
10. Ibid., 367.

it facilitates mapping the development spatially and temporally. Even accounts that mark a moment in Greek thought as the beginning of philosophy acknowledge that this beginning occurred in a context in which other things were already happening. Attending to what and where as well as when may be an aid in understanding this beginning.

In describing the African background and foundation of Greek philosophy, Henry Olela focuses on Sais, an ancient name for what the Greeks rechristened "Egypt." (Faulkner describes it as an ancient city in the North Central Delta, cult center of Neith, the creator-goddess.) He identifies four "schools" by the cities with which they were associated: Heliopolis, Hermopolis, Thebes, and Memphis. Olela asserts that the "Memphis" school shaped Greek (and hence Western) philosophy.[11]

Olela briefly outlines the philosophy of two schools, Heliopolis and Memphis: Heliopolis placed Atum-Ra (the Fire God) above everything else, describing it as "self created." This school named four other gods or "elements":

Shu (Air)

Tefnut ("opposite" of Shu, responsible for world order)

Geb (Earth)

Nut (Sky)

Shu and Tefnut were known as children of Atum-Ra, Geb and Nut as grandchildren. Before anything else was created, there was Nun, a primordial abyss of water. Memphis altered the order somewhat but kept many of the elements:

Nun (water)

Ptah (a hill)

Atum-Ra (sat on the hill)

Tefnut (world order)

The Memphis school (like the one at Heliopolis) arranged the gods into a set of "opposites":

Nun (Water)	Naunet (Heavens)
Huk (Boundless)	Hauhet (Limited)
Amum (Visible)	Amaumet (Invisible)

11. Olela, "African Foundations of Greek Philosophy," 43–49.

Kuk (Darkness) Kauket (Light)

Olela describes a complex picture of "soul" and "body": Ba is Soul, Ka is a "double," Khu is a "Shining" part that bridges the gap between human and divine, and Khat is Body. Ba has physical characteristics, so libation and food are offered. Ka is a "conceptual" replica of spiritual reality. The "intellect" remains in Ka after death.

Finally, Olela proposes a partial list of equivalences between elements of Egyptian philosophy and the Presocratic philosophers:

Thales	water	Nun
Anaximander	boundless	Huk
Anaximines	air	Shu
Xenophanes	one god	Ptah
Heracleitus	fire	Atum
Anaxagoras	nous	Khu

Pythagoras: "mathematical" via Orpheus?

Parmenides: one/spherical earth

Democritus: atomic system

In a moment, I will turn to a more detailed description of individuals within this group designated as "Presocratic" and to the significance of the designation. For now, though, I want to focus on the equivalences themselves. The first six denote correspondences between *archai* (first principles) in Greek philosophers and Egyptian deities. It's important to bear in mind that naming a deity is a time-honored way in many cultures of naming what is "really real" and hence what is the basic "stuff" of the universe, and that is at least one way of reading what is going on here in both Egyptian and Greek contexts. The last three denote less precise correspondences in the form of shared ideas and/or probable influences.

Martin Bernal's argument in *Black Athena* is helpful in thinking through how these related but historically and geographically distinct ways of talking about what is "really real" might fit together. Bernal argues that the "Ancient Model" regarding classical civilization, which traces the origins of "classical" Greek civilization (including philosophy) to Africa, has deep roots and affirms especially Phoenician and Egyptian origins of Greek thought. His evidence includes references to Egyptian colonies in Thebes and Athens and other parts of Greece and the Phoenician foundation of Thebes. He offers evidence against claims made in the nineteenth and twentieth centuries that the "Ancient Model" was concocted late (fifth century BCE). We will return to these nineteenth- and twentieth-century claims later as instances of containment strategies grounded in fear of difference. More important for now is the invention of difference, particularly the cultural decision regarding which differences make a difference. Bernal takes us to the heart of one of the most important arguments in the West over precisely that question. Bernal's first concern is to offer evidence of the historical depth of what he calls the "ancient model," which locates Greek thought against a background that is Egyptian and African (though don't lose track here of Mudimbe's argument that Africa is being invented as a container for Egyptian thought even as the West is emerging to contain Greece). He draws on a number of different kinds of sources, including a play (*The Suppliants*) by Aeschylus, which describes the arrival in Argos of Danaos and his daughters and which employs a vocabulary that shows significant Egyptian influence. He suggests a pun between *hikes(ios)* (suppliant) and Hyksos. He also cites one of Plato's dialogues, the *Timaeus*, which assumes a close connection between Egypt and Greece, particularly between Athens and Sais, and which was the most influential of Plato's works through the Middle Ages. He takes the fact that traditions of colonization which implied a derivative (or inferior) position for Greek culture were transmitted by that culture as evidence that the traditions are substantially true—assuming, with some justification, I think, that the inclination of Greek (and other) cultures is to suppress such traditions. If the assumption is correct, such traditions survive only where they are strong enough to resist tendencies toward suppression. In any case, there doesn't seem to be any good reason for a culture to concoct such traditions.

Like Olela, Bernal also points to equations between Greek and Egyptian deities and the widespread assumption that the Egyptian forms were older. This, he suggests, accounts for the widespread worship of Egyptian deities under Egyptian names in both the Greek and the Roman world. Only with the collapse of Egyptian religion in the second century CE was the Egyptian religion replaced by other "Oriental" cults, including Christianity.

Bernal describes a process by which the Church Fathers "tamed" Egyptian religion, transforming it into a philosophy identified with Hermes Trismegistos, a rationalized version of Thoth (the Egyptian god of wisdom). The Church Fathers were divided on whether Hermes Trismegistos was earlier than Moses and the Bible, but they were in agreement that the Greeks learned their philosophy from the Egyptians—whom they suggested may have learned some of theirs from Mesopotamia and Persia. Throughout the Middle Ages, Bernal asserts, Hermes Trismegistos was seen as the founder of non-biblical philosophy and culture. This belief continued through the Renaissance, when there was a revival of interest in Greek culture but an almost equally passionate interest in Egypt. The consensus was that the Greeks learned from the Egyptians, and Bernal suggests that the attempt to recover Egyptian wisdom lay behind some of the Renaissance advances in science and philosophy (he refers, for example, to Newton). The Hermetic texts were important for the Neoplatonist movement. Bernal goes on to suggest that the revival of interest in the Egyptian concept of a divine sun was one impetus for Copernicus's heliocentrism.

He points to the seventeenth and eighteenth centuries as times of continued Egyptian influence. Influential European thinkers of the eighteenth century preferred Rome to Greece because they saw the former as a model of order; but they also looked to Egypt and China as alternatives to the Greek past. Both Egypt and China were seen as having superior writing systems (representing ideas, not sounds)—and both were admired for their rational governments. Bernal notes that the appeal of Egyptian priesthoods had deep roots in the West. Plato modeled his guardians after them (in the Republic), and this line of thought was taken up by the Freemasons (who were politically and intellectually quite influential) in the eighteenth century. (Take a look at Mozart's opera "The Magic Flute" for concrete evidence of the influence.) One way to think about this is as a search for what Van Wyck Brooks referred to as a "usable past."[12] In a present where order is a particular concern, a past that provides a foundation for such order is useful to those seeking it. Notice that the order being sought is always a particular order and that talk of "good old days" (both formal and informal) is almost always a strategy for criticizing (and an argument for transforming) "new" days that are not so good.

Hostilities to Egypt became pronounced in the eighteenth century. Newton's attitude toward Egypt shifted from one of respect to one of dismissal—Bernal suggests that this is a result of the threat posed by pantheism to his "orderly" universe. This is a tension that has been critical in the invention of the West, which has equated its drive toward order with

12. Brooks, "On Creating a Usable Past," 337–41.

a monotheistic turn. We will return to it. By the middle of the eighteenth century, there was a pronounced tendency to use the idea of "progress" to maintain that later is better. This, too, is an important tension in the invention of the West, which has positioned itself between myths of a golden age and myths of progress. The idea of progress led to an elevation of the Greek culture and civilization and a downplaying of the older Egyptian civilization: the development of Greek thought was identified with progress. Bernal also notes that the diminishment of Egypt coincided with the rise of racism in the West.

Bernal suggests that India became more prominent in the late eighteenth and nineteenth centuries partly because of a perceived connection between Sanskrit and European languages. European expansionism was connected with a changing image of both China and Egypt. Where they had been seen as orderly and rational, they were increasingly recast as disorderly and "unclean." Bernal explicitly connects the rise of racism and colonialism with the changing image of Egypt:

> Another way of looking at these changes is to assume that after the rise of black slavery and racism, European thinkers were concerned to keep black Africans as far as possible from European civilization. Where men and women in the Middle Ages were uncertain about the colour of the Egyptians, the Egyptophile Masons tended to see them as white. Next, the Hellenomaniacs of the early 19th century began to doubt their whiteness and to deny that the Egyptians had been civilized. It was only at the end of the 19th century, when Egypt had been entirely stripped of its philosophic reputation, that its African affinities could be re-established. Notice that in each case the necessary divide between Blacks and civilization was clearly demarcated.[13]

Bernal asserts that the "Ancient Model" declined in influence between 1790 and 1830 as a result of racist and Christian opposition to Egyptian influence. It was increasingly replaced by an "Aryan Model" which identified Greece as the cradle of civilization. Proponents of the Aryan model were also unabashed proponents of the idea of "progress." Conquerors were seen as more advanced, those conquered as more primitive. History came to be pictured as the victory of the strong and advanced over the weak and primitive. This was increasingly associated with the mythology of a master race later identified with Hitler. That identification led to its

---

13. Bernal, *Black Athena*, 30.

partial discrediting after the Second World War, when it was replaced by a "Broad Aryan Model" that Bernal suggests is still in force. This model admits especially Semitic influence, but still tends to downplay the role of Africa in general and Egypt in particular.

Bernal's argument is of particular interest to us because it suggests in a striking way the extent to which historical accounts function as "foundation myths" for political and other communities. They often serve to answer the questions "Who are we?" and "Where did we come from?" and are therefore driven by a desire to separate that means some stories will be heard and others not heard. This does not mean that we should dismiss historical accounts, but reading them with this in mind may help us read them more critically: one can never include everything, so a crucial question for philosophy (or any other discipline) is what is (and/or ought to be) included. That question is not always asked explicitly, but it is always answered in practice. As readers, we can make some important critical judgments by becoming aware of what is not included in any particular account as well as what is.

"Western" philosophy is almost always described as having been born in Greece, so that accounts of its "origins" are almost invariably accounts of the philosophical tradition of ancient, particularly classical, Greece. This is true on both sides of Bernal's argument, where the difference of opinion involves not the origin of philosophy but its relevant background. The earliest cosmological and cosmogonical speculation in Greek, essential to understanding the philosophical tradition that blossomed in Plato and Aristotle, predates the classical period by several centuries and is found in the work of Homer and Hesiod, dating probably from the seventh and eighth centuries BCE (though extant written versions are much more recent). All of this speculation comes to us in specifically "poetic" form, most notably in Homer's epic *Iliad* and Hesiod's *Theogony*.

Traditional accounts often credit Thales as the first philosopher (and also, from time to time, the first astronomer), but the earliest of those accounts suggest either that he did not write at all or that he wrote in epic verse. In any case, nothing survives except a few citations in later authors. The situation is not much better for the whole class of philosophers somewhat misleadingly lumped together under the title "Presocratic." The title is misleading not in terms of its timeline but in terms of its singularity. What this group of philosophers, including Thales, most definitely have in common is that they predate Socrates (though the latest of the group,

Democritus and Diogenes, are his only slightly older contemporaries). Beyond that, they are a decidedly diverse group.

What is most revealing about the title, perhaps, is that it follows Plato in designating Socrates as the single most important watershed in philosophical history: like the birth of Jesus, the Hijra, and the creation of the world, Socrates is seen in "the West" as an event by which all other events may be dated.

The Presocratics drew heavily on the "poetic" accounts of Homer and Hesiod as well as the "mixed" account of Pherecydes. They cited poets freely (though not always explicitly), and often (as in the cases of Xenophanes, Parmenides, Empedocles, and—perhaps—Thales) themselves wrote poetry. Of the eighteen authors (from Thales to Diogenes) included in Kirk and Raven's collection, five (Melissus, Philolaus, Eurytus, Archelaus, and Leucippus) left so little direct evidence as to render it virtually impossible to assess their style of writing (though it is possible, as Kirk and Raven amply demonstrated, to make rather substantial deductions regarding its content). Of the remaining thirteen, two (Thales and Pythagoras) probably didn't write at all (though, as noted above, some sources suggest that Thales wrote epic verse, and Pythagoras's mystical "theological" bent is so well known as to require no further comment here). One (Heracleitus) probably didn't write a book, certainly not in the form of a connected narrative, but spoke (and perhaps wrote) in *gnomoi*, "carefully formulated opinions" or aphorisms that amount to riddles. Another (Zeno) devised paradoxes that, though not poetry, are also not simply straightforward prose. Two (Anaximenes and Anaximander) wrote in prose but with language and imagery described by their successors as "poetic." That leaves a total of four (Democritus, Diogenes, Anaxagoras, and Alcmaeon) who wrote in what could be designated "simple" prose.

If this selection of Presocratics is expanded to include Homer, Hesiod, and Pherecydes, all of whom engaged in important cosmological and cosmogonical speculation before Socrates, the blurring of any supposed line between poetry and prose is even more pronounced—so pronounced, in fact, as to raise the question of why these particular thinkers are so often set apart from others as philosophers. Aristotle had some rationale for setting them apart as *physikoi*, thinkers particularly concerned with *physis*, "nature" (though that category could most certainly also include Homer, Hesiod, and many of the "lyric" poets including Sappho). However, the "Western" tradition has never been inclined to limit the category of "philosopher" to "natural philosophers," as is confirmed, for example, by Socrates, who focused much of his attention on moral matters.

That there is in many cases considerable controversy regarding whether a particular Presocratic philosopher wrote at all is further evidence of their affinity with poets. Socrates was suspicious of books and, at least in the portrait passed on to us by Plato, did not write them. To the extent that Socrates is the real watershed by which "Western" philosophy measures itself and the world, philosophy (like poetry) is, at its origin, an oral discipline: Socrates, like Homer, "sang" divinely inspired words.

Plato seems to have only reluctantly resorted to writing them down (i.e., in the Greek sense, becoming a poet). His well known distrust of poets is an indication that he shared his predecessors' faith in the power of words. What made them powerful also made them dangerous. Socrates and some of his predecessors appear to have responded to this danger by avoiding the written word, preferring the more malleable and more organic spoken form. Plato responded to this danger by suggesting that poets and poetry be kept on a short leash. He was certainly convinced of the power (both political and educational) of a good story and seems to have been convinced that one political function of the philosopher was to properly discriminate between "good" stories and "bad" ones.

In "the West," that Platonic distinction increasingly came to mean discrimination between "true" stories and "false" ones. To the extent that "the West" (as a fictional heuristic device more attentive to history than to geography) is tied up with the emergence of Roman Christianity as a successor to the Roman Empire, the discrimination of "true" stories from "false" ones is a history of the identification and suppression of "heresies," increasingly identified (at least until the Reformation) as "Eastern." It is probably not coincidental that many of the best sources for fragments of Presocratic philosophy are polemical treatises written against various Greek heresies.

That it is common practice to identify Thales as the "father" of "Western" philosophy is revealing. Thales was Greek, a citizen of the Ionian city of Miletus, but some of the earliest available sources (sparse though they may be) describe him as Phoenician by birth. Whether one accepts those sources at face value or not, it is undeniable that the context of Thales' life and work was not Greece itself—certainly not Athens—but a Greek-speaking enclave on the edge of the Medean, then-Persian, world. This enclave was a commercial center where any "educated" person would be exposed to many cultural influences, particularly those associated with Asia Minor. If "Western" philosophy was born with the emergence of the *physikoi*, then its lineage is not only "Greek" but also Semitic and "Persian."

But this lineage, which must be broadened to include Africa—particularly Egypt—predates the *physikoi* by many centuries. The earliest cosmogonical accounts in Greek, given written form by Hesiod (and, to a lesser extent, by Homer) in the seventh or eighth century BCE, include an earth encircling river, *okeanos*, that was probably borrowed from the older civilizations of Egypt and Mesopotamia, which depended on one or more rivers (the Euphrates, the Nile, or the Tigris) for their very existence. There are certainly echoes of the Sumerian/Babylonian and Egyptian cosmogonies in Hesiod's account, which, like Homer's, reflects (and to some extent "systematizes" or "inscribes") a long "popular" oral tradition. Just how deep this "popular" tradition ran is suggested by the extent to which first Hesiod and Homer and then Thales and his successors could simply assume it. The image of an earth-encircling river appears to have been so widespread as to make it possible for Thales to look "naturally" to water as the source of all things. This appears to have been as natural for Thales as for the anonymous thinkers of Mesopotamia and Africa who first "sang" the visions. In fact, there appear to have been several cosmogonies that originated in Mesopotamia and/or Africa that provided the "natural" material for the reflection of the *physikoi*. In addition to the earth-encircling river that inspired Thales, there were stories that emphasized earth, air, and fire. The succession of Presocratic (particularly Milesian) *archai* familiar from Aristotle's Metaphysics reads like a collection of *midrashim* on these stories.

I have already mentioned Thales, whose Phoenician roots and physical location on the coast of Asia Minor gave him easy access to Mesopotamian cosmogonies (such as that in the *Enuma Elish*) that are rich sources for speculation on earth, air, and water as origins of all things. That he chose water as *archos* is consistent with the cosmogonical tradition inscribed by Hesiod. Anaximander, who was a near contemporary of Thales, drew on the same sources to suggest the enigmatic *apeiron*, "boundless." His student and successor Anaximenes continued the "midrashic" tradition, shifting attention from water to air as the source of all things. Kirk and Raven credit Anaximenes with introduction of the word *psyche* for both breath and wind, a usage that later became common with the tragedians. In Aristotle's account, Heracleitus, born in Ephesus (also in Asia minor) around 540 BCE, continued to ring the changes in search of an *archos*, offering fire as an alternative to water and air. He criticized other thinkers for what he called collection of disconnected "facts," insisting on the connection rather than the "facts" themselves as the "point" of reflection. He appears to have pictured reality as a huge fire that "inhales" and "exhales" equal amounts in an unending unity of opposites that appears on the surface as a struggle. The similarity to early concepts of Agni on the Indian subcontinent and the significance of fire in the Zoroastrian system that became the state religion of Persia under Cyrus, during Heracleitus's lifetime, is striking—so striking as to make it almost inconceivable that there was no direct influence. At the very least, Heracleitus would have been familiar with the tradition of the *Gathas* and Zoroaster's vision of cosmic struggle within eternal unity. The "Milesian" thinkers who are almost always credited as the first Greek philosophers show a marked Asian and Mesopotamian, particularly Zoroastrian influence. I would go so far as to suggest that, if this is the first stage of Greek (and, by extension, "Western") philosophy, then the "first" stage is really a second order process of commentary on "sacred" texts that have their ultimate origin not in Greece but in "the East."

A similar case could be made for the development of the Pythagorean and Eleatic systems of Presocratic thought, which took place (again) "on the margins" of Greece, this time on the Italian peninsula. In the religio-mystical tradition of Pythagoreanism, there is a marked Egyptian influence, sometimes apparently by way of Orphic tradition. The religious poetry of Parmenides (and the later poetry of Empedocles) bears striking resemblance to "Eastern" speculation taking place at about the same time in the early stages of Buddhism. Without straining to make a physical connection between Parmenides and India, suffice it to say that there were some common "themes" in the air and that reflective speculation on those themes took a form (whether in Italy or in India) that was both poetic and religious. In this regard, it is important to bear in mind that, from the perspective of China, India is West. Chad Hansen and others have argued that India should be included in the intellectual construction of Western thought as distinct, especially, from Chinese thought.[14]

It is, of course, undeniable that the origins of the Hellenes are as thoroughly entangled with Asia Minor as with Greece. The great epics

14. Hansen, *Daoist Theory of Chinese Thought.*

out of which the concept of Greece (or Hellas) was born are war stories centered on a struggle with Ilium (Troy) that transformed twelfth-century Mycenaean warlords like Agamemnon into the heroic forbears of Greek civilization. That transformation was itself intertwined with a centuries-long process by which the Trojan War was recast as a battle between Europe and Asia. There is reason to believe that, without the Persian threat (projected back into the Trojan threat by historians like Herodotus), there would have been no occasion to think of Hellas at all. The pivotal role of Athenian naval power in the later struggles against the Persians made it possible for increasingly self-conscious Greek (read Athenian) writers to make Athens the center of Hellas, the Hellas of Hellas, at the same time that "philosophical" and literary activity moved from "the periphery" toward the Athenian center: the Athenian invention of Greece seems to have hinged on a particular construction—an invention—of Persia as well.

This is an interesting precursor of the long process that Mudimbe and others have described as "the invention of Africa." The "West," he has argued convincingly, constructed itself at least in part by constructing Africa as "other," beginning as early as Herodotus but taking shape most dramatically with the emergence of the Roman world. Aeneas's treatment of Dido, read against the backdrop of Rome's struggle with Carthage, is a case in point.

The "geographic" process by which first Greece, then Rome, then the West were constructed in the invention of "others" (whether Persians, Africans, *barbaroi*, *agrioi*, or *oiorpata*) is intimately connected to the construction of disciplines (by which first "philosophy" then "science" are set apart from "poetry" and "theology" and accorded special status) and the construction of canons (by which "true" stories are set apart from "false" ones).

It certainly is the case that terms such as *barbaroi* and *agrioi* were extant as early as Homer in Greek literature. But the social process of their definition is coterminous with the emergence of Athens as the Hellas of Hellas and is more important than their existence at the beginning of that literature. From the beginning, they function as names, categorical distinctions that draw a line between those who live in the city and those who don't. That line is older than the Greek language, as evidenced, for example, by the *Epic of Gilgamesh*; and it is instructive. Cities play a crucial role in the construction of both history and geography. In fact, histories of the "West" almost always begin by designating the Sumerians, the first builders of cities, as the dividing line between "prehistory" and "history," and maps almost always begin by picturing what is not "city" as empty. *Agrioi* is one of several terms that function to distinguish "us" from "them," and in the Homeric universe, this has the important effect of drawing a circle that includes both Ilium and the "Greek" city-states while it excludes those who do not live in cities. This is one reason why it is possible for Homer to paint an often sympathetic picture of the Trojans even as he depicts them as engaged in life and death struggle with the "Greeks." It may also be what makes the "Greeks" appear progressively less "civilized" as the time they spend outside the city is protracted by the war. *Barbaroi* draws a different circle, one that divides the Trojans from the Greeks on the basis of language. This is the beginning of a hierarchy that is of profound importance for the invention of "the West." It designates those who speak "our" language and live in "our" city as most human, those who speak "our" language but live in "other" cities as less human, those who speak "other" languages and live in "other" cities as less human still, and those who live "outside" the city and speak "other" languages as little better than animals (who, it should be noted, live "outside" both the city and language, except in the case of domesticated animals which have historically complicated the hierarchy).

It is not surprising that this process of division is thoroughly intertwined (I am almost tempted to say coterminous) with religion. In the emergence of a Greece centered on Athens, where the most salient feature is the invention of Persia as "other," it is instructive that two famous trials of philosophers, that of Anaxagoras and that of Socrates, hinged on the charge of "impiety." In the case of Anaxagoras, one source expands "impiety" by suggesting that the accusation was "impiety and Medism," which we might read as "worshiping the gods of the other." I take this as evidence for the influence of Persian thinking on "Greek" (and thus "Western") philosophy. "Medism" was present from the time of Thales (and before), but it seems to have become a problem in the peculiar construction of "Greece" that defined Athens at the time of the Peloponnesian War. That is to say that (whether the charges against Socrates and/or Anaxagoras were trumped up or not) "Athenocentrism" had become the standard by which "true" stories were distinguished from "false" ones: anything that threatened Athenian hegemony was, by definition, impious.

Plato's ambivalent relation to this development is reflected, I think, in his distrust of poets and his defense of Socrates. He seems not to have disputed the Athenocentric construction of history, though his Spartan sympathies (and his brief experiment with politics in Syracuse) suggest that he blamed Athenian "democracy" for the disintegration of Greece (which is practically indistinguishable from the execution of Socrates in his account). For Plato, as reflected particularly in the *Republic*, the only legitimate act of *poiesis* is the construction of the "true" city: the "poem" that constructs a true city is a "true" story, and all others are "false."

I have no doubt that Plato's conclusion was dangerous, but I am not entirely convinced that it was wrong.

That it was dangerous is reflected (paradoxically) in the expulsion of Anaxagoras and the execution of Socrates. It is also reflected in the Alexandrian "cosmopolis" that came a generation after Plato, perhaps in part due to influence that he exercised through his student Aristotle, at least to the extent that this "cosmopolis" was constructed on the assumption that the "true" city would be born when the whole world was recast in Alexander's image. It is reflected in the ease with which those who have claimed Plato as intellectual forbear have built "true" cities on the backs of "others" who, as "others," have been rendered instrumental and expendable. The relationship of Europe with Africa for most of the past five hundred years is a case in point, as is the whole tradition of European (and Euro-American) colonialism. The "invention" of Persia, both in an Iranian and an Iraqi manifestation, in the recent history of the United States, is also a case in point.

That it is not wrong (at least not entirely) depends on the extent to which the vision of a "true" city remains open, to the extent that the "true" city is posed as problem rather than *idée fixe*. Aeneas, as founder of Rome (and ultimately of "the West") proceeded on the assumption that the founding was at the same time necessarily the abandonment of Dido and the murder of Turnus. But philosophy does not have to make that assumption and, in fact, dies when it does.

Certainly, the assumption is part of the legacy of "the West," and it is a part of that legacy that, though it must be remembered, is, to borrow a phrase from Toni Morrison's *Beloved*, "not a story to pass on" . . . Baby Suggs, a character—one of the wisest characters—in that novel, observes elsewhere that good consists in knowing when to stop and that white people (i.e., "the West") don't know when to stop. Like Plato, Morrison values both story and truth. In Baby Suggs, one of the truest of her characters has rediscovered the importance of limits and starting places that were so much on the minds of seekers of wisdom in the Greek-speaking world before Socrates.[15]

Cities (or civilizations), like stories, become destructive (they become false) when they do not know or do not remember when to stop. Virgil constructed an Aeneas who was virtuous enough to hesitate when confronted by Dido and Turnus. Our mistake, I think, has been to define Aeneas as virtuous when he plunges ahead rather than seeing the more transitory virtue that recurs in his moments of hesitation. That virtue— the one that flashes in fits and starts through his hesitation—although it was not enough to stop Aeneas or save Dido and Turnus, is worth cultivating as we join our ancestors in the search for wisdom.

15. Morrison, *Beloved*, 123.

PART TWO

Recurring Nightmares

4

Recurring Nightmares (Four Themes)

I DESCRIBED the case studies in chapters 2 and 3 as schematic, intending thereby to emphasize the need to expand and fill in gaps. The same is true of this chapter, in which I will briefly introduce four themes to which we will return in subsequent chapters. My intention here is not to provide an exhaustive paradigm or to exhaustively describe the suggestive paradigm I do propose. I take Hountondji's point about the openness of philosophical inquiry seriously. What I suggest here is a heuristic device, an aid to vision. Like the raft that gets us across the river, it should be abandoned if and when we reach the other shore.

Having said that, I remind you of the point I made near the beginning, that histories of ideas are material histories. Because they are (as long as we humans are narrating them) human histories, their materiality consists in "nature" that includes both biological and cultural transformation. These are not mutually exclusive categories: culture is biological, and both are natural. This contradicts a substantial portion of "Western" philosophy in which nature and culture have been presented as diametrically opposed. It is important to be aware of both the traditional presentation and the claim I have just made as arguments—not dispassionate descriptions, but passionate engagements in a controversy that matters. The heuristic framework that follows begins with that materiality. I will describe the themes in what I understand to be the chronological order of their emergence in human development (though evidence is sketchy enough to render any order imposed on the account speculative). This is not meant to suggest that subsequent themes supersede earlier ones. It would be more accurate to think of the themes as levels that build on one another and recur together beginning in prehistory and continuing throughout human history, recognizing that there is inevitably considerable controversy about the order in which they surface.

Language and Perception

The theme I place first is that of language and perception. I put it first because it is fundamental to human history as a reflective process. It begins with the emergence of language among primates, probably some forty thousand years ago, probably in a region of northern Africa that is part of modern Ethiopia. Like many developmental lines, this one is fuzzy, as evidenced by the genetic proximity of human beings to other primates—especially chimpanzees and bonobos—and by the symbol-manipulating capacity of other primates. Historically, some theorists have invested great energy in distinguishing human beings from other primates on the basis of language, but I believe it is a waste of energy to try to make that distinction sharp or absolute. I am not even convinced that the distinction between primates and other animals is a necessary one; although humans far outdistance other primates in symbolic capacity and primates outdistance other animals, symbol manipulation in communication does not appear to be limited to primates. What is necessary, I think, is attention to the development of symbolization, which provides the basis on which language develops (in the further transition from symbol to sign). Language in turn forms the basis for history not only as a reflective process but also as a shared, public one.

Human language development has been understood as progressing from orality toward literacy, and there is much to commend that view (as well as the modification made by some theorists that would extend progression through literacy to post-literacy). I suggest that we broaden it a bit, though, and think in terms of development from transitoriness toward portability. I emphasize *toward* portability, since language is always transitory, and the ability to transport it is always limited spatially and temporally. It is tempting to speak in terms of development from immediate toward mediated communication; but all communication (and all language) is mediated. The evolution of language is an evolution of media. The earliest language consists of gesture (including sound), which has an obviously limited range. The range of a physical gesture may be limited by touch: I can, for example, communicate by putting my hand on your shoulder—but the range of that communication is only as long as my arm. If you move beyond arm's length, you move out of range. It may also be limited by vision: I can communicate by waving at you or tipping my hat—but the range of that communication is only as long as your ability to see. If I am out of sight, my wave or tip of the hat will not communicate to you. It may also be limited by hearing: I can communicate by saying "hello" or *ni hao*—but the range of that communication is only as long as your ability to hear. If I am out of earshot, my "hello" will not communicate a greeting to you. Obviously, each of these gestures is subject to physical limitations other than distance. If you are within arm's length but behind a plexiglass barrier, I cannot put my hand on your shoulder. Even if you are close enough to see me, my tip of the hat or wave will not communicate if you are behind a wall. I may be quite close to you, but if I take my glasses off, I will not see you tip your hat. If you put on a surgical mask to protect yourself from a virus, I won't see your smile (though I may extrapolate it from your eyes). And if a truck roars by as I say "hello," you may not hear me even if I am standing right next to you.

All of this indicates why various technologies can revolutionize language. If I have a webcam or a videophone, the distance from which I can wave at you is greatly extended (though it is still not unlimited, and there is room for argument about whether I am present to you if what you see is an image on a video display). The same is true if I amplify my voice or transmit it via telephone or radio. Touch is a bit more problematic in this regard, isn't it? If you create a robot that mirrors your actions at a distance, I probably will not experience the robot's touch as equivalent to yours—though that could be debated, and some people would argue that this, too, could be addressed technologically. If the robot is sufficiently "lifelike," it might serve the purpose, though I suspect that I would then feel the robot's touch, not yours; but that is a subject for another discussion. Technologies can extend the spatial range of gestures, but that alone does not make them portable.

Portability requires that temporal range be extended as well, as, for example, in writing. The development of written language, then, probably some fifty-five hundred years ago, is another milestone in human development, and it is often considered to be the dividing line between "prehistory" and history (though that involves an argument about the interpretation of artifacts, doesn't it?). In individual development, it is also considered to be an important milestone: the division between literacy and illiteracy is a significant one in terms of power and social standing. Notice that this, too, is a matter of technology and that it requires two kinds of development. First, gestures have to be transformed into representations; and, second, those representations have to be sufficiently standardized to allow for (more or less) unambiguous interpretation. Instead of tipping your hat, you can draw a picture of a tipped hat. If I know it's from you, it will communicate a greeting as long as the paper (or whatever you've drawn it on) and the ink (or whatever you've drawn it with) survive. Note that this introduces more technological dimensions. Cave walls are durable, but not transportable. Clay tablets are transportable, but they are easily broken. Bones last a long time, but they take up a lot of space. These are all factors to consider in thinking about media.

Sometimes we get confused here, because we focus exclusively on writing. But what we are really talking about is recording. Every means of recording and transmitting gestures is potentially a revolution in communication. This is true of painting on cave walls as surely as it is true of audio and video recording devices.

So, language develops from unrecorded to recorded gesture, and, in the process, it becomes increasingly transportable. But a sender's gesture is only as good as a recipient's ability to understand it. Some gestures are pretty unambiguous, others less so. And ambiguity tends to be partly a function of culture: nodding your head up and down does not mean the same thing everywhere, for example—nor does the hand on the shoulder that I mentioned earlier. This points to a second way in which language develops—and, in fact, pointing is exactly the right image: language development moves from pointing through symbolizing toward signifying. With that development, both communication and potential miscommunication are enhanced as the gesture becomes conventionalized. We move from a picture toward something that, by convention, stands in for the picture. And this is an interesting moment in the history of the "West."

Historically, the first written language is pictographic: we find pictures on cave walls, for example, that predate all other written records. What happens to it next is the subject of some controversy. One way of describing what happens is to move from pictographic writing through ideographic writing to alphabetic writing. That, I think, is a progression most likely to be advocated by those who see their own language as primarily alphabetic (often the same people who see their alphabet as phonetic). I would suggest, though, that the alphabet is a peculiarly "Western" way to make the representational move from picture to idea (associated historically with the Phoenicians and, via its name—alpha + beta—with the Greeks, who adopted it from the Phoenicians). It seems pretty clear that this is one reason (as was noted earlier, in discussion of Bernal) for changing attitudes in "the West" toward Egyptian and Chinese writing systems. Leibniz, for example, believed that the Chinese writing system was superior to European systems precisely because it represented ideas rather than sounds—this in spite of the fact that it was already customary by the time he wrote to depict the Phoenician alphabet as an advance over Egyptian hieroglyphics. But the question of superiority is, it seems to me, misguided. The strategies are different, and each has its own strengths and weaknesses. The choice may have far-reaching cultural significance, so it merits the kind of careful attention Leibniz gave it.

I said earlier that the evolution of language is an evolution of media, but the progression just outlined suggests a modification. The evolution of language is an interplay between evolution of media (or means) and refinement of both purposes (or ends) and methods. It is also important to clarify that use of the term "evolution" to modify media is not meant to impute superiority to later over earlier media. A minidisc recorder, for example, is not intrinsically superior to a pencil, and neither is intrinsically superior to charcoal pigment and a horsehair brush, but each carries strengths and limitations. Learning to use a pencil may be easier than learning to use a brush, for example; so the pencil may increase the number of people who are able to record. It's also less messy and, therefore, perhaps more likely to be used. Operating a minidisc recorder requires no particular skill, though it does require access to electricity and is relatively more expensive. Perhaps, then, it is better to think of transformation rather than evolution of media: evolution of language is an interplay among transformation of media, transformation of ends, and transformation of methods. New methods, new ends, and new media separately or in any combination transform language; and all have served the evolution of communication in human historical development. Here again, a caveat is in order with regard to "evolution." Communication has not gotten unequivocally "better" with the transformation of methods, ends, and media, though it has certainly changed. Whether communication is better when everyone has a cell phone in their back pocket than when they are sitting around a campfire telling stories is debatable.

But for now, the point is to trace at least some of the changes and their associated differences as a first step in considering the difference the differences make. It appears that oral language develops first, out of a more general capacity for symbolization that human beings share with other primates (and perhaps with other animals as well). It develops sequentially from index (pointing) through symbol to sign—from motivated to unmotivated or conventional, as Piaget put it, following de Saussure. (This raises an interesting question, though, for comparative psychology. My cat, arguably, understands symbols better than she understands indexes. If I point at her food, it means nothing to her; but if I shake the container, she knows food is forthcoming. Taking that one step further, if I ask her in the morning whether she wants breakfast, she gets up, stretches, and usually vocalizes a response. Does that mean she understands signs as well as symbols, but not indexes? If so, the developmental sequence may have to be modified: pointing may be more complicated than we thought.) Written language emerges later, but there is considerable controversy over whether it develops out of oral language. The two are clearly related, often directed toward the same end; but how they are related is a complex question. In the United States at the time I am writing, some politically influential theorists argue that oral language is "natural" (by which they mean that it does not have to be taught) while written language is "artificial" (by which they mean that it requires direct instruction). The distinction is, to say the least, simplistic. Both oral and written language are cultural; and, as I asserted earlier, culture is biological. (What is culture about if not *bios*, life?) I think it makes most sense to think of the two as distinct but related aspects of culture, both intimately connected with communication, and both intimately connected with means (media) and ends. One of the reasons, for example, that the capacity of humans to learn human languages is superior to the capacity of chimpanzees is that humans have vocal cords equipped to make sounds that are building blocks of human languages, while chimpanzees do not: we have access to a medium that is unavailable to chimpanzees. This is why primate language researchers shifted their attention early on from trying to teach chimpanzees to talk to teaching them sign language, for which they have far greater physical facility. By the same token, primates (including human beings) are physically incapable of the kind of communication in which dolphins appear to routinely engage. The ways in which we communicate, then, depend partly on the media available to us. If our ears are limited to a frequency range of 20–20,000 hz (and, given the wear and tear on our ears, an even smaller range—particularly at the upper end), communication is limited to that range (unless the ears or the messages being communicated are technologically modified).

Oral language depends on the vocal cords and the ears, and it probably developed simultaneously with other gesture languages; so-called "sign language," for example, depends on the hands and the eyes. It is certainly possible to imagine communication systems based on any combination of sensory mechanisms. (Virginia Woolf, for example, wrote a biography of Elizabeth Barrett and Robert Browning's dog Flush in which he communicated much more by smell than by hearing or vision—a fact that anyone who has spent any time around a dog is likely to confirm.[1]) The development beyond gesture or pointing toward symbol or picturing is probably associated both with the development of the first forms of written language and with the development of greater complexity in all language. It is not unreasonable that greater language complexity went hand in hand with expanded media. And it is hardly surprising that greater complexity depended at least in part on greater cognitive capacity (another factor in the language-learning ability of human beings as opposed to other primates). I would suggest that oral language developed from gesture to symbol at the same time that pictographic written language developed. It is not a matter of one developing out of the other, and it is certainly not a matter of one being more "natural" than the other. It is a matter of two forms of language developing as the capacity for symbolization was employed for purposes of communication. Referring to pictographic language privileges vision, and that connects us with an old argument. For the moment, I want to avoid the argument by suggesting that there is no particular reason to privilege pictures over other symbols. My cat, for example, is no more likely to respond to a picture of food than to my pointing at food. She is, however, likely to respond to a representation of food in sound or smell. In her case, then, pictures are less effective symbolic representations than sounds or smells. She would not get excited if I presented her with a picture of a bird, but she wakes from a sound sleep

1. Woolf, *Flush*.

every time I play a recording of Charlie Mingus's "Cumbia & Jazz Fusion," which begins with bird sounds. We can argue about music as language, and we can argue about what (or whether) Mingus was communicating when he included those sounds at the beginning of this recording, but my cat responds to the sounds pretty much the same way she responds to a bird on the windowsill. For her, the sounds function very effectively as symbols. For me, too: I think "bird" every time the recording starts.

The next step—from symbol to sign—is perhaps more interesting. Any means of communication can conceivably be conventionalized in various ways to convey ideas rather than gesture toward objects. A picture of the sun, for example, might come to represent light or day or the god Aten. The picture, perhaps, "looks" like the sun (though that is a stretch, isn't it?)—but it doesn't look like light or day or (presumably) Aten. A picture can be connected by convention with all sorts of things that it does not resemble. Likewise a sound. Those birds on the Mingus recording might just as effectively evoke daybreak as a picture of the sun. And what about a rooster crowing? Daybreak? The liberation of Zimbabwe? The point is that we can collectively disconnect the image from representation of an object while simultaneously connecting it with evocation of an idea or a concept. In written language, this can be accomplished effectively by combinatorial systems that are primarily ideographic as well as by systems that are primarily alphabetic. Alphabetic systems depend more clearly on connection with spoken language, and that may be understood either as a strength or a weakness. The point, though, is that both ideographic and alphabetic strategies move language away from motivated symbols toward conventional signs—and both do it by creating and elaborating systems to convey ideas rather than simply gesturing toward objects. Means that facilitate such conveyance are important to cultural development. In Chinese, calligraphy is such a means—and the development of brushes and durable inks as well as techniques for using them is of critical importance. Block printing is a revolutionary development, because it enables mechanical reproduction of a single act of calligraphy. Alphabetic languages can also make use of block printing, and even better use of an invention like movable type. In the history of the West, the emergence of that technology in fifteenth-century Germany probably made the difference between the local impact of Hus and the global impact of Luther, though another way to read that would be that movable type made it possible for Luther and those associated with him to extend Hus's impact to global proportions more quickly than the authorities in Rome could extinguish it. Taking another step backward, Hus's impact was facilitated by the availability of Wycliffe's ideas in the form of a printed book, and the printed book was carried to Bohemia by disciples who had heard Wycliffe speak. If speaking is the only means by which to convey ideas, the ideas can be silenced by killing the speakers before they inspire others to speak. If the ideas are also conveyed by books, they can be slowed or stopped by burning them before many people have had a chance to read them (or by limiting the number of people able to read). The more people speaking, the harder it is to kill them all. The more people reading, the harder it is to keep them from turning into people who are speaking. So expanding literacy and technologies that facilitate dissemination of ideas both have revolutionary potential. In this regard, the fax is at least as important to the twentieth century as movable type was to the fifteenth. The same may, of course, be said of cell phones and the internet.

Though I identified this first theme as language and perception, what I have said so far is concerned almost entirely with the former. I group the two together for a number of reasons that I hope will become clearer in subsequent chapters. First is one that has already been mentioned in passing: language development takes the directions it does at least in part because of the perceptual interfaces available to us as we interact with the world around us. We interface with the world via eyes, ears, nose, mouth, and skin—sight, hearing, smell, taste, and touch.

The correspondence thus enumerated is misleading, because the senses are not contained in the organs with which they are identified. Each is a complex system that also includes nerves and brain, and all interact—sometimes in surprising ways. The line between smell and taste, for example, is notoriously fuzzy—and tasting one thing while smelling another can be a confusing experience. Less obvious is the fuzziness of the line between vision and taste, but test it by following Dr. Seuss's lead: dye your eggs green, and see if their taste is unaffected. Good cooks are well aware of this: if food doesn't feel right or look right, it won't taste right either; and attractive presentation can go a long way toward covering unappealing taste. The cosmetics industry would have us believe that something similar is true of interpersonal relations, and, given the size of the industry, it appears to have convinced quite a number of consumers.

But the situation is further complicated by the fact that there are two sets of complex systems interacting here, and there are ongoing debates concerning how to describe the sets, the systems that comprise them, and their interactions. One debate concerns the independence of the sets. If one set is the world and the other the (human) organism, it seems self-evident that the first set contains the second. In this case, all interactions between the sets are internal to the world, some are external to the organism, and some are internal to the organism. Perceptual systems internal to the organism come into contact (via sensory organs) with systems external to the organism (including other organisms). From the perspective of the organism, this may be understood as an interaction of "inside" with "outside," and "knowing" may be understood as an "accurate" correspondence between the two. From the perspective of the world, there is no outside, and it makes little sense to speak of "correspondence," though it may make sense to speak of complex interactions among subsystems—or of harmony among subsystems. But where is all of this "making sense" taking place? One influential stream of Western thought has argued that it takes place in mind, which is not, strictly speaking, part of the (physical) world. In this case, one set is the world and the other set is the mind (or the soul); mind or soul is, perhaps, imprisoned in world, but its *raison d'etre* is to escape that prison by abandoning it, transforming it, or transcending it. Mind, then, is understood as (ideally) not being contained by body—and certainly not being contained by brain. It is often understood as being an entirely different kind of thing (*res cogitans*, in Descartes' version) distinct from the physical (*res extensa*). This is an interesting trick, because it places one kind of thing while arguing that another kind is placeless—placing it no place, as it were. This tradition has had far-reaching repercussions for the way human beings think of themselves and their place in the world—particularly in the "West." One way of responding to it is succinctly summarized in Marvin Minsky's assertion that mind is what brains do. This (accurately, I believe) identifies the separation as a category confusion. When category confusions are hardened and essentialized, they become particularly destructive. We will return to this—at least in part because I believe returning to it over and over again has been characteristic of "Western" thought.

Death, Identity, and Mortality

In terms of chronology, it would probably be more precise to say that the second theme—death, identity, and mortality—emerged simultaneously with the first. The remains of the earliest humans show evidence of funerary practices—suggesting a consciousness of death—that are as old as language itself. This is perhaps itself an artifact of definition: to find evidence of funerary practices, we need some sort of record; the existence of a record of funerary practices is itself an instance of symbolization. So, we encounter the two hand-in-hand—in the form of remains buried with implements needed for daily life, which we read as pointing toward belief in continuation of daily life beyond death.

Of course, that is circular; and it may tell us more about our interpretive processes than about the beliefs of early humans. But some of the oldest stories that have survived in written form revolve around questions of death, mortality, and identity. *The Epic of Gilgamesh* is an example of an extended narrative dealing with these issues, and the *Egyptian Book of the Dead* gives evidence of very early ritual practices associated with a belief in continuity beyond death. Hebrew Scripture turns almost immediately to the question and even appears to connect death with the emergence of human consciousness associated with moral choice. In this account, human beings emerge from the earth, animated by God's breath. But they become conscious of their own responsibility for choosing good or evil at the same moment they become conscious of death as something they will necessarily confront. Socrates, at the very beginning of Greek philosophy, demonstrated his "heroic" stature in the way he faced death—one of the reasons that the French philosopher Miguel de Montaigne would write in the sixteenth century that to philosophize is to learn to die. Montaigne may have learned this from Plato's Socrates, but Plato learned it from Greek tragedy, which represented the confrontation publicly and repeatedly.

The widespread adoption of "Eastern" religions—particularly Christianity and Mithraism—at the birth of the Roman West was driven partly by the promise of resurrection those religions carried. The way that promise was developed in Christianity still shapes Western concepts of death and identity. One of the most important ways in which this theme has been developed in the West has been in reflection on the Christian ritual of the Eucharist, particularly in the long controversy regarding God's presence in that ritual.

God and the World

The third theme, God and the world, is related to the second by way of Eucharistic theology. Stating it in this way (with the singular God capitalized as though representing a proper name) is to give it a comparatively late "Western" slant. But, as has already been suggested, the struggle behind that slant is of primary interest; it has generally taken the form in the West of a movement from polytheism toward monotheism, spectacularly demonstrated in Akhenaten's abrupt shift in Egypt around 1345 BCE and in the more gradual shift that occurred several hundred years later in Hebrew belief. The long "conversion" of "barbarian" Europe to Christianity often looked like a battle between polytheism and monotheism; and that tension—even where it has been secularized—continues to fuel Western debates on issues such as multiculturalism. Because the earliest antecedents of the West identified gods with forces and places in nature, struggles of human beings against natural forces were often depicted as struggles between human beings and the gods. This is true as early as the *Gilgamesh Epic*, and it is a recurring theme in Greek and Roman literature (as in the *Odyssey* and the *Aeneid*). Struggles between human beings were often depicted as struggles among gods—sometimes on two levels, as in Euripides, sometimes in an interpenetration of levels where struggles among gods could also be struggles between human beings (some of whom—Aeneas and Achilles, for example—were understood as being partly divine) and gods. The interpenetration of divine and human is a common theme in the West, from the giants of Genesis through the divine/human Greek heroes and deified emperors of Rome through the birth of Jesus. With the rise of Christianity, there is a drive to separate human and divine—to keep the divine "holy"—that is in almost constant tension (spectacularly in interpretation of the Eucharist) with the drive toward interpenetration. The rise of Islam is partly a reaction to that tension. Islam intensifies the separation, identifying "association" of anything with God as idolatrous, and reading Christianity as corrupt to the extent that it encourages such association, particularly in its understanding of the incarnation.

Christian Monasticism, Islam, the Inquisition, the Crusades, and the Reformations (both "Protestant" and Catholic) are all driven in part by a desire for purity that—for better and worse—has marked the West. Monasticism grew in the aftermath of martyrdom in the early church and was connected with a missionary impulse that was often difficult to disentangle from a military impulse. Islam accuses its predecessors of corruption and association, narrating its own history as a return to pure submission to God. The Inquisition accuses elements within Christendom of heresy and corruption and seeks to purify itself by eliminating the corruption.

This reaches a fever pitch in Spain with the *reconquista* and the expulsion of Jews; but it is mirrored, particularly in anti-Semitism, throughout Europe. The Crusades, as I have already mentioned, turn outward toward Islam—but also toward "Eastern" Christianity and the "barbarians" of Lithuania. The Reformations, from Hus through Luther and Ignatius to the Campbellites, narrated competing histories in which the narrating communities contrasted their pure practice of original Christianity with the corrupted practice of other Christians and of infidels.

When George W. Bush said "you're either with us or against us," he drew on a long and deeply rooted "Western" tradition.

Civilization and the Shape of the City

The fourth theme, related to each of the first three, is civilization and the shape of the city. The identity of the West is so thoroughly entangled with the idea of "civilization" that it can be understood from the beginning as variations on the theme of foundation. The *Iliad* is about a war with Troy, the city of Asia Minor, but it is also the story that makes a Greek civilization out of competing Mycenean warlords. The *Aeneid* cleverly adopts a survivor of Troy as the founder of Rome and makes the foundation of Rome simultaneously the murder of Turnus, representative of the indigenous peoples of the Italian peninsula. Christian missionary activity, embodied in monasticism, is identified with the Romanization of Europe, then the Europeanization of the whole world. Even before Greece and Rome, the question of the city emerges (as early as Sumer) as a tension between rural and urban, local and global. This relates to the first theme, language, because the question is often which language: in the West, this has come in linguistic waves—Indo-Aryan, Greek, Latin, Arabic, Russian, English. Civilization—citification—has often taken the form of centralization in waves of expansion: Alexander the Great, the Roman Empire, Christianity, colonialism, "settler" civilizations in the United States and Southern Africa, the Soviet Union, NATO, the European Union, the World Trade Organization. This is not simply to equate these waves, but it is to call attention to a common thread that runs through them— centralization and globalization in tension with local identity and local sovereignty. That tension defines the "civilization" of the West. It is related to the third theme's drive toward purity, since it often proceeds by identifying and containing "others," within and without. The "city" of the

West is a narrative defined at least in part by the murder of indigenous peoples (from the Canaanites through Turnus, the Wends, the Taino, the Cherokee, the Sioux, the Xhosa, the Ndebele . . .) and at least in part by internal oppression in the form of inquisitions, heresy trials, pogroms, and witch hunts—literal and figurative.

5

The Nature of Nature

THAT I believe it is a mistake to label Aeneas's plunging ahead as a virtue and strength, his hesitation as weakness and vice, does not, I am afraid, alter the fact that we—the West—have done so and continue to do so. This has been true, for example, in our construction of heroes. (In the *Iliad*, Achilles assumes heroic proportions because of rage that drives him to prowess on the battlefield and causes readers to forget his sulking— also rage-driven—at the beginning of the epic. Jesus, too, was transformed quickly from suffering servant to *pantokrator*, ruler of the universe.) It has also been true in our construction of "reason" as instrumental—specifically, as an instrument of conquest. (Odysseus, for example, is cast as heroic, not sneaky, when his stratagems get him where and what he wants.) In the construction of the West, conquest has often been figured as conquest of nature, and it has almost always been gendered. In the case of both Achilles and Aeneas, the struggle has been cast as an internal one in which wrath can serve to "emasculate" (and the sexual connotation of the term is a key factor in my choosing to use it) or to invigorate. Whether a character is heroic depends on whether he (or she) turns anger to action (figured as masculine) or passion (figured as feminine). Women who become heroes in this tradition do so by becoming "honorary males," and the heroic martyr is recalled for his/her action—not for reflective hesitation.

Genevieve Lloyd begins *The Man of Reason* (with reference to Beauvoir and Nietzsche) by noting a long-standing "Western" tendency to construe rational knowledge as "a transcending, transformation or control of natural forces" and to associate the feminine "with what rational knowledge transcends, dominates or simply leaves behind." Beauvoir associates "male activity" with an overcoming of "the confused forces of life" that has "subdued both Nature and woman." Nietzsche asserts that "woman's closeness to Nature makes her play to the State the role that sleep plays for man." Lloyd begins, then, with two analogies that have been influential in "Western" thought:[1]

> female : male :: Nature : culture
>
> woman : State :: sleep : man

Greek thought, she argues, was predicated on the assumption that "culture" was to be constructed in opposition to "nature" and that this construction would proceed by means of "reason." Reason was associated with the male and nature with the female. Plato, she notes, asserted that women imitate the earth. The implication is that men imitate the heavens—and that "civilization" is a process of ascent from earth to heaven by means of reason. As she notes, this was expressed mythically in relation to the oracle at Delphi, where Apollo broke the power of the Earth Goddess with the assistance of Zeus. This echoes mythic accounts in other cultures, including those of the Middle East (Marduk slaying Tiamat or Yahweh slaying Leviathan, for example). Even though the indigenous warrior (Turnus) slain by Aeneas to found Rome was male, he was identified with the earth—and it was Aeneas's own "feminine" hesitation that was slain when he sunk his spear into Turnus's chest.

The Pythagorean table of opposites, Lloyd tells us, associated the female with the unbounded, the vague, the indeterminate, the male with the bounded, the precise, and the clearly determined. She lists ten contrasts:

limited	unlimited
odd	even
one	many
right	left
male	female
rest	motion

1. Lloyd, *Man of Reason*.

straight	curved
light	dark
good	bad
square	oblong

These were not simply "descriptive" categories: those on the left were seen as superior to those on the right on the basis of a "primary" contrast between "form" and "formlessness."[2] Again, there are echoes of this all around the "Greek" world, one of the most familiar being the creation accounts in Hebrew Scripture, where God imposes form on a formless universe by speaking.

In later Greek philosophical thought, this series of distinctions was taken up in an association of maleness with "active, determinate form" and femaleness with "passive, indeterminate matter":

form	matter
male	female
active	passive
determinate	indeterminate

In describing Plato's epistemology, Lloyd asserts that knowledge consisted of a correspondence between rational mind and rational forms. Reason permeated the world in much Greek thought, but for Plato this was the case only with respect to form. The identification of rational thought with a rational world was achieved only by transcending matter and seeking a connection between the (rational) form of the world and the (rational) form of the mind. Knowledge consists of (in)forming the mind to match the form of the world.

In the *Timaeus*, Plato set up another important analogy:

world-soul : world :: rational soul : body

This is important for Lloyd because of the pervasive association of "maleness" with reason, which tilts the analogy toward an association of the soul of the world with the male; but it is also potentially important because it depicts the world as a living—ensouled—organism.

Lloyd depicts a progression in Plato's thought from a simple dichotomy between body and soul to a more complex dichotomy between reason and the non-rational within the soul itself. In both forms of the

2. Ibid., 3.

dichotomy, though, Plato picks up a mythic image of ascent from the human toward the divine by means of reason. That image played an absolutely crucial role in shaping subsequent philosophical and theological speculation in the West.

It is important to bear in mind that Plato's hierarchical model envisioned a domination within the knower: the point is to bring the body (and bodily desires) under the control of the mind (and spiritual desires). As Lloyd notes, this hierarchical model with its imagery of domination was transformed in the West (particularly by Francis Bacon) into a hierarchical model in which the knower dominated the known. Knowledge gradually came to be associated with domination. (Remember the discussion of "love" in chapter 3: *eros* is directed toward possession while *phileo* is directed toward community. Lloyd recasts this as a distinction between domination and contemplation. This is not unjustified, particularly since the ensouled earth of Plato's *Timaeus* is more like a divinity worthy of "enraptured contemplation" than a fellow creature and potential friend.)

Plato, Lloyd suggests, progressed beyond the Presocratics in that he distinguished "formal" principles from the "material" ones they sought in their various *archai*. He associated the "formal" with the permanent and unchanging, the "material" with the impermanent and changing. Reason was directed, as we've already noted, toward identification with the formal—the permanent and unchanging. All of this may have contributed to a tendency to tilt philosophy toward an escape from the material world: matter is an illusion that distorts one's vision of the real.

Aristotle collapsed the distinction. The permanent, unchanging form is encountered only in impermanent, changing matter. And so Aristotle directed attention toward concrete universals: matter is not an illusion that distorts one's vision of the real so much as the place where one encounters the real. This shift was later refined by Aquinas, but, as Lloyd notes, the shift does not eliminate the form/matter distinction. Knowledge still consists of an abstraction of form from matter, even if this is done in encounter with each material object rather than in escape to a realm that is free of matter.

Bacon completed the collapse of the distinction between matter and form, transforming knowledge from contemplation to control of Nature. There is an almost complete reversal in the more than two thousand years that separate Plato and the Presocratics from Bacon. Where Plato's understanding of knowledge consisted of (in)forming the mind to match the form of the world, Bacon's consists of mastering the world by making it conform to the human mind and human will. As the Baconian understanding of knowledge as control comes to dominate Western thought, science increasingly becomes a matter of making the world in our image.[3]

This transition was associated with an abandonment of the Platonic (and Egyptian) understanding of the world as ensouled organism in favor of an identification of the world entirely as matter devoid of soul. To put the best construction on Baconian efforts to control nature, one could suggest that he saw the task of the knower as being to "ensoul" (or humanize) a nature that would otherwise be soulless. I suspect that this is also related to a tendency associated with Christianity to transform the soul into an exclusively human characteristic. To the extent that this transformation was complete, the only way to ensoul something would be to "humanize" it or transform it into a human form.

Lloyd suggests that the "theme of the interconnections between knowledge and power is Bacon's main contribution to our ways of thinking about mind's relation to the rest of Nature."[4] We'll have occasion to return to that theme more than once—particularly when we turn with Cornel West to examination of the pragmatists and Foucault.

Given our concern with "mapping" philosophy, we should bear in mind that the geographical and historical shift of philosophy from Africa and Mesopotamia through Greece toward northern Europe and specifically England in the genealogy implicit in our reading so far has involved a collapse of the distinction between the "theoretical" and the "practical" that has—in Bacon—also collapsed the distinction between "knowledge" and "utility." This is emphatically not a simple transformation from speculative to practical knowledge. (Remember that the knowledge associated with *sophia* in Greek was practical knowledge, and think of the close association of architectural and agricultural practice with speculation in Egypt.) It is, however, an extended conversation (or argument) regarding what constitutes knowledge. Bacon explicitly associates knowledge with power and power with control. (Again, that is not unique, since the same sort of association is pervasive in the practice of magic.) What is perhaps most uniquely "English" in this conversation is the association of

3. Not coincidentally, this involves a transformation from the passion of philosophy to the action of science. One could construe the Latin *scientia* as a translation of *sophia*, thereby making the disappearance of *phileo*—passion—explicit.

4. Ibid., 13.

control with utility and profit. That association would be one way to map the philosophical schools that emerged in the English-speaking world of the seventeenth, eighteenth, and nineteenth centuries. That it would be an historically useful map could be tested with reference to Bernal. I suspect you would find a rather marked correspondence between the emergence of Baconian science with its associated attitudes toward technology and the construction of both Greece and Egypt in European thought.

Philosophical arguments about nature and what is "natural" in the West are often explicitly—and almost always at least implicitly—theological. This is the flip side of my earlier discussion of the philosophical significance of explicitly theological arguments—particularly those of the Egyptian and Mesopotamian cultures that informed the Mediterranean context in which Greek philosophy—and Western thought—began. In this regard, it is important to pay particular attention to Genevieve Lloyd's claim about knowledge and power. She is hardly alone in making this claim (which is often associated with Foucault), but she traces its implications with particular clarity. This is why I turn to her argument as an aid in thinking through the long conversation about what constitutes knowledge and how it is related to both power and control. Lloyd is quite right, I think, to plumb the conversation for its impact on construction of gender. But it is also important for its impact on constructions of power relationships—particularly as related to will and control—more generally. This conversation in the West took on a theological dimension with lasting cultural significance: is "order" established by God's arbitrary act, or does God act in accordance with a preexisting—necessary—order? This theological question has had far-reaching consequences for "Western" understanding of human action and human knowledge.

Lloyd describes a development in Plato's thought from an early conception of the whole soul as the domain of reason standing in opposition to the "non-rational body." In this model, the life of reason is a rejection of bodily desire. (Note the influence that this conception of reason and its relation to the body had—and has—on the ascetic tradition in Christianity.) This early conception was replaced, Lloyd tells us, with a more complex model of division between rational and non-rational elements within the soul itself.

This development in Plato's thought is associated with a refinement of his conception of reason. Lloyd asserts that "the later Plato . . . saw passionate love and desire as the beginning of the soul's process of liberation through knowledge; although it must first transcend its preoccupation with mere bodily beauty, moving through a succession of stages to love of the eternal forms."[5]

Lloyd recounts Diotima's teaching regarding love (which, you will recall, is one of the constituents of philosophy—*phileo*) in the *Symposium*. The pursuit of wisdom, she says, is a spiritual procreation connected, like physical procreation, with "a desire for immortality through generation." The "art of love" (more specifically, the "art" of philosophy) is a progression from love of the particular to love of the general, from earthly beauty to "absolute" beauty. Note that this is an envelopment (remember Hountondji) that moves out from a physical center like ripples from a pebble dropped in water at the same time that it is an ascent. For Diotima, the "ascent" is a movement from the "physical" to the "spiritual" that proceeds along with the movement from the "particular" to the "general." Note, too, that both the envelopment and the ascent involve a fusion of the good, the true, and the beautiful. This should alert us to an understanding of philosophy that will include both action and passion as well as thought.

Lloyd's treatment of Philo focuses on the application of Plato to the creation accounts in Genesis. It is an interesting case study in the "fusion" of cultures that has played such an important role in the development of philosophy in "the West." Here Philo embodies the Hebrew and Greek strands of the tradition in his method of Scriptural interpretation. This method was to have a profound influence on Christian interpretation of Scripture as well. Here again, it is worthwhile to remember Hountondji, particularly his discussion of philosophy as a "second order" discourse. Philo, like his Egyptian predecessors, constructs his "second order" philosophical discourse in the process of reflecting on sacred texts.

Lloyd is also concerned with the slippage between literal and symbolic interpretation of the texts. In particular, she notes Philo's appropriation of an already well-established "Western" tendency to associate femaleness with the bodily and maleness with the spiritual. Although she charitably suggests that it was not Philo's purpose to exclude actual women by drawing a picture of spiritual ascent that moves from the female to the male just as Diotima's ascent moved from the physical to the spiritual, it is not hard to see how the exclusion would follow as a direct result: He doesn't exclude women; he just encourages them to become "honorary males"(!).

5. Ibid., 21.

Augustine, Lloyd asserts, strongly opposed association of female subordination with "lesser rationality."[6] Beginning with Christian commitment to spiritual equality, Augustine set out to reinterpret the Genesis accounts in a way that countered the misogynism of earlier interpretations (including Philo's). The issue for Lloyd revolves around Augustine's attempt "to articulate sexual equality with respect to Reason, while yet finding interpretative content for the Genesis subordination of woman to man."[7] The result is that bodily difference comes to bear the symbolic weight of difference in Augustine's interpretation: "spiritual" equality or equality with respect to reason is distinguished from "physical" inequality. In spite of his greater sensitivity, Augustine constructs an argument that has much the same effect as earlier associations of male and female with soul and body: it legitimates a subordination of women that is taken to be "natural."

Just as Philo serves as an excellent case study in the synthesis of Greek and Hebrew strands of "Western" tradition, Augustine serves as an excellent case study of the further transformation of that synthesis in transition from Judaism to Christianity. Philo's Genesis is a Jewish text; Augustine's Genesis (though it is the same text) is a Christian one. That is instructive in terms of reading philosophy (including philosophical reflection on sacred texts) as a history.

The Greek tradition is represented in Philo and Augustine by Plato. As Lloyd notes, it is represented in Aquinas not only by Plato but also by Augustine's Plato and by Aristotle. (It is interesting, by the way, that the Aristotle to which Aquinas had access had been preserved and filtered via Arabic and Islamic commentators. This is further evidence of the multicultural matrix of "Western" philosophy—even where that matrix is not consciously acknowledged.)

Aquinas, Lloyd argues, derived a more integrated view of human nature than Augustine's from his reading of Aristotle. Of particular importance is the idea of "substantial form as the intelligible principle of a body. The intellectual soul is the form of a living human body." This has the effect of making "body" and "soul" inseparable, with soul being understood as body's form. Given the "Western" association of male with soul and female with body, it is not surprising that this "integrated" view would have profound implications for understanding relationships between men and

6. Ibid., 28.
7. Ibid., 29.

women. The body, Aquinas might well suggest, is no less real than the soul: but without the soul it is dead. (We will return to this issue of the body, which has been a sore spot in Western thought, as we have already seen in Plato's Socrates.) This is further complicated by Aquinas's adoption of the Aristotelian concept of principle "as that from which operations flow." For Aquinas, God is the principle of the whole universe, and the first man (in God's likeness) is the principle of humanity. Aquinas moves toward an analogy with profoundly negative implications for women:

> God : Man :: Man : Woman

This hierarchical understanding is not entirely new in "Western" thought, but Aquinas has carried it further than his predecessors, and his interpretation will have a profound influence on the conceptions of domination and control carried further still in Bacon.

At the very end of chapter 2, Lloyd notes that philosophical thought about Reason has involved the "genderization" of "ideals of rationality": "An exclusion or transcending of the feminine is built into past ideals of Reason as the sovereign human character trait. And correlatively . . . the content of femininity has been partly formed by such processes of exclusion."[8] Lloyd's account of this whole progression is a cautionary tale depicting the political and ethical impact of ontological speculation: It is not just "femininity" that is formed by processes of exclusion associated with "philosophical" speculation.

Lloyd begins her third chapter with reference to Hegel, who is representative of a tendency in Western philosophy to associate "maleness" with "reason" and attainment. She is particularly concerned with the seventeenth-century development associated with Descartes that defined reason as a method, a skill that could be learned.

Method is associated in Greek with a road or path to be followed. This idea was developed by Plato's Socrates in the *Phaedrus* as involving processes of generalization and division. We are admonished to divide at the joints and to be aware of the relationship between parts and the ends or wholes toward which they are directed.

Lloyd argues that Descartes transformed method as a reasoned path, a reasoned way of proceeding, into a way of reasoning: the path itself is identified with the act of reasoning. The identification and description of this path in Descartes is thoroughly entangled with his separation of

8. Ibid., 38.

mind and body. For Descartes, the method of arriving at Truth is separated from methods and procedures of public discourse. Truth becomes an individual, abstract process rather than a concrete public (and political) one. Lloyd associates Descartes' mind/body dualism with the shift toward individualism in the seventeenth century as well as the shift toward a conception of reason associated with attainment.

That Descartes' intentions were egalitarian is reflected in the fact that he wrote his *Discourse on Method* in vernacular French rather than Latin, thus making it available to a larger audience and violating a line that had been drawn by the use of Latin to distinguish the educated from the uneducated.

That the effect of his "method" was not egalitarian is a result, Lloyd argues, of the history of association of maleness with mind, femaleness with body—and of the impingement of the "ordinary" world of everyday activity on the "life of the mind." To the extent that the social construction of gender gave women responsibility for the everyday activities that freed men to cultivate the disciplines that Descartes associated with "reason," it excluded women from the life of reason.

Lloyd asserts that Hume develops the Cartesian version of reason by maintaining that it has "no power to control passion or deliberate about ends." The motivating force of reason lies outside itself in "the driving force of passion." The effect of Hume's argument is to stand seventeenth-century rationalism on its head: our knowledge resolves into expectations of stability and predictability that arise from "customary associations in the mind."[9]

Lloyd is most concerned with the moral and political implications of Hume's argument. He moves from the passivity of reason to the primacy of passion, then argues that political structures must be constructed in such a way as to facilitate the restraint of (some) passions by (other) passions—as opposed to restraint of passion by reason. According to Lloyd, this leads Hume to advocate enlightened self-interest, a sort of "calm" as opposed to "violent" passion, as the basis for politics and morality. Lloyd describes this as a substitution of "reflective passion" for reason.

Lloyd summarizes the relationship in Hume:

> This, then, is Hume's version of the relationship between Reason and passion: immediate self-interest subjected to the control of

9. Ibid., 52.

a higher and more reflective version of itself. Reason in its 'improper' sense—whether it be 'calm' as against 'violent' passions, 'reflective' as against 'immediate' and 'partial' self-interest, or 'remote' perspective embodied in magistrates as against the pursuit of short-term interests—controls passion. And this relationship of dominance or control is articulated in terms of a distinction between 'public' and 'private' interests. The public passion of acquisitiveness is given the role of curbing private interest in acquiring goods and possessions for the sake of the individual and his family.[10]

Her conclusion is that the implications of Hume's philosophy for gender construction and relations between men and women, though unintended (or unstated), are nevertheless far-reaching. Given Hume's comment about custom "concealing itself," I suspect the implications are more far-reaching because they are unstated.

When Lloyd turns her attention to the "optimism" of the Enlightenment, she first examines Rousseau's dissent. Contrary to the myth of uninterrupted progress, Rousseau depicts a "corruption" of humanity coinciding with the "progress" of civilization. He sees human society both as the source of human misery and (properly constructed) as the source of human ennoblement. This poses the serious question of how to "properly construct" human society. Rousseau shifts attention from Bacon's concern with the character of the good scientist to concern with the character of a good citizen. He proposes that reason should be held in check by nature, not the other way around.

Lloyd summarizes Kant's contribution with a phrase from his essay "What Is Enlightenment?": dare to know. Enlightenment consists in emergence from self-incurred immaturity and is therefore not only an attainment but also a form of maturation. This maturation takes the familiar form of development from particularity toward universality (though Kant's critical philosophy keeps the progression open by probing the limits of human reason).

Hegel carries this trend toward universalization to its extreme at the same time that he unites nature and reason in the embrace of an Absolute unfolding of Spirit in the world. Lloyd refers to Hegel's statement in *The Phenomenology of Spirit* that "womankind is constituted through suppression." This has become an important source for philosophical reflection

10. Ibid., 55–56.

on the experience of oppression and double consciousness. Lloyd connects it with the progressive disjunction of "public" and "private" realms that began to accelerate with Descartes. She traces the disjunction from Rousseau through Hegel, in whom the distinction between "public" and "private" is developed alongside a distinction between "inner" and "outer." The "outer" is the realm of "actuality," while the "inner" is insubstantial and finds its reality only through externalization or "objectification." Hegel identifies woman with the "inner" and "insubstantial" at the same time that he identifies the fully human with the "outer" and "actual." Men are assumed to have access to this "outer" realm and are therefore able to become fully human. Women are relegated to the "inner" realm and denied full humanity.

In Lloyd's conclusion the central question is again a question of power.[11] In Hegel's philosophy, womankind is constituted by (male) containment. Lloyd describes Beauvoir's "ideal for women" as being that "they should themselves break away from the 'immanence' in which they have been . . . contained, to achieve their own transcendence—the state of self-definition and self-justification—through freely chosen 'projects and exploits.'"[12] Lloyd sees Sartrean and Hegelian roots for this argument, though I think it is historically and philosophically more accurate to see the roots in a dialogue carried on between Beauvoir and Sartre vis-à-vis Hegel and the "Western" philosophical tradition.

In tracing the Hegelian roots of Beauvoir's account, Lloyd notes that, for Hegel, self-consciousness "demands inter-subjective awareness. An isolated consciousness cannot sustain self-consciousness."[13] The "positive" interpretation of objectification in Hegel consists in the presentation of consciousness to itself as object—hence the Hegelian interest in "externalization" (and its connection to the concept of "project" in Beauvoir and others). In Hegel, this is developed especially in his discussion of the slave-consciousness (in *Phenomenology of Mind*). As Lloyd puts it, "through forming and shaping things, the slave's consciousness acquires what eludes the master—an element of permanence; he [or she!] discovers himself [or herself] in the forms his [or her] work imposes on objects."[14]

11. Ibid., 85.
12. Ibid., 87.
13. Ibid., 88.
14. Ibid., 92.

Sustained self-consciousness demands externalization of the self in action (and more specifically in the act of production, which is also an act of making public).

Sartre's analysis of the metaphysics of the gaze argues that "we cannot perceive as an object a look fastened on us; it must be either one or the other. To apprehend a look directed at us is precisely not to apprehend an object; it is, rather, consciousness, of being looked at."[15] The Sartrean "other" is "the one who looks at me." The Sartrean self, Lloyd asserts, is a constant struggle to break free from the "fixing" of the self by the gaze of the other.

Lloyd argues (at the end of chapter 6) that "transcendence" itself—at least as it is articulated in Hegel and Sartre—is not gender neutral. She seems to be pushing us toward a rethinking of the concept of "transcendence" itself (and its association with reason). This also means a rethinking of the concept of "objectification" and the significance of embodiment for our knowing (and our acting) in the world.

In her conclusion, Lloyd points to a pervasive distortion of concepts of reason associated with a systematic exclusion of women from their articulation. This poses an important problem for rethinking the concepts and the process of their articulation (a problem that bears a striking similarity to the one noted by Hountondji in his discussion of African philosophy). Lloyd concludes that

> philosophers can take seriously feminist dissatisfaction with the maleness of Reason without repudiating either Reason or Philosophy. Such criticisms of ideals of Reason can in fact be seen as continuous with a very old strand in the western philosophical tradition; it has been centrally concerned with bringing to reflective awareness the deeper structures of inherited ideals of Reason. Philosophy has defined ideals of Reason through exclusions of the feminine. But it also contains within it the resources for critical reflection on those ideals and on its own aspirations. Fortunately, Philosophy is not necessarily what it has in the past proudly claimed to be—a timeless rational representation of the real, free of the conditioning effects of history.[16]

Like Hountondji, she concludes with an important reflection on the history of philosophy (and philosophy as history):

15. Ibid., 94.
16. Ibid., 109.

to highlight the male-female distinction in relation to philosophical texts is not to distort the History of Philosophy. It does,
however, involve taking seriously the temporal distance that
separates us from past thinkers. Taking temporal distance seriously demands also of course that we keep firmly in view what the
thinkers themselves saw as central to their projects. This exercise
involves a constant tension between the need to confront past ideals with perspectives drawn from the present, and, on the other
hand, an equally strong demand to present fairly what the authors
took themselves to be doing. A constructive resolution of the ten-
sions between contemporary feminism and past Philosophy requires that we do justice to both demands.[17]

It is important, I think, in reading both Hountondji and Lloyd, to
bear in mind that the tension itself may well be more important than its
resolution. Where Beauvoir speaks of "project," she may have in mind
the construction of self and world that takes place in the tension between
"past" and "present." The temporal distance that Lloyd speaks of is a dimension of the "space" in which we live (and in which we do philosophy).
One way of approaching this philosophically is to see the future (as possibility) breaking into time and transforming both "past" and "present." The
Kantian interest in "possibility" and "necessity" (best articulated, I think,
in Piaget) then makes some sense as a space in which our "projects" are
undertaken, in which we become the subject of those projects rather than
simply the object of an other to whom we are nothing more than "other."

17. Ibid., 110.

6

Real Presence

ANNE Conway is at the center of a philosophical map Leibniz sketched in a 1697 letter to Thomas Burnett—midway between Democritus and Plato, holding Descartes at arm's length with one hand, Henry More with the other:

> My philosophical views approach somewhat closely those of the late Countess of Conway, and hold a middle position between Plato and Democritus, because I hold that all things take place mechanically as Democritus and Descartes contend against the views of Henry More and his followers, and hold too, nevertheless, that everything takes place according to a living principle and according to final causes—all things are full of life and consciousness, contrary to the views of the Atomists.[1]

Leibniz was a consummate mapmaker—not surprising for a philosopher whose thought was above all relational. I begin this chapter with one of the many maps he drew, employing it as an aid in locating Conway, a less well known seventeenth-century philosopher of internal relations. Conway has been rescued from obscurity by reference to her work in Carolyn Merchant's *Death of Nature*, by recent translations of her philo-

---

1. Cited by Carolyn Merchant in *Death of Nature*, 257. The complete correspondence [in French] is contained in the third volume of Leibniz's *Philosophischen Schriften*.

sophical notebooks, and by a number of articles that have examined her influence on Leibniz's monadology. The influence itself is hardly a matter of dispute—as evidenced by Leibniz's own acknowledgment. Its extent has been a subject of some controversy, but it is not of particular concern here, and I will turn to it only briefly in what follows. I return to Conway not because I think Leibniz borrowed from her or because I think of her as a "proto-Leibniz" but because I think her fragmentary work is an important development of Cambridge Platonism and one foundation for a philosophy of internal relations that is not Hegelian. My primary interest here is not Leibniz but his map, which I take as a finding aid in picking up a thread of thought Conway wove out of a number of materials, including, most notably, Platonism's Cambridge variety.

The 1697 letter was written two years into a nineteen-year correspondence that is most memorable for its insights into Leibniz's reading of John Locke. Some champions of Leibniz have read Merchant's discussion as diminishing Leibniz's philosophical importance by attributing influence to Conway, van Helmont, and, indirectly, More. This led Stuart Brown to argue that, because Leibniz misread More's relationship to Kabbalah, his reading of More and those associated with him could not have been more than casual and that references to these philosophers in the correspondence with Burnett were intended to soften the blow of critical comments on Locke with favorable comments on other prominent British philosophers. But Leibniz selects philosophical references with care and makes a number of fine distinctions among More, van Helmont, and Conway that elevate Conway to a position of particular importance. Though she was honored by her contemporaries, it would be surprising for anyone writing in the seventeenth century to single out her work rather than the work of a better known (and male) contemporary merely as a courtesy. Something in Conway's philosophy commended it to Leibniz, particularly in his reading of Locke and particularly in his effort to make himself understood by a British correspondent conversant with (and critical of) Locke.

If, as Gilles Deleuze suggested, Leibniz was "God's attorney," he was an attorney who favored out-of-court settlements, whose style was more diplomatic than adversarial, whose philosophy was negotiated—not conquered—territory.[2] He was not only God's attorney but also God's diplomat, and the map unfolded in his letter to Burnett bears the marks of a territorial settlement. Bertrand Russell was less kind than Deleuze in his reading of

2. Deleuze, *The Fold.*

Leibniz, criticizing him for having two contradictory philosophies—a private one grounded in logic and a public one rendered irrational by its subservience to officially sanctioned theological dogma. Whenever he spoke rationally, Russell asserted, Leibniz tended toward Spinozism—so he made it a habit not to speak rationally in public. Russell's reading of Leibniz's logic, though interesting, has been thoroughly criticized; his public/private division, which has been less thoroughly criticized, is of greater interest, because it sheds some light on the location of Leibniz's philosophy.

Russell expected to find this philosophy in a system and was put off by its fragmentary and dispersed appearance in correspondence. He contended that commentators on Leibniz would first have to construct the system he should have built out of the fragments he embedded in correspondence, then criticize the system. Fascinating though this construction and criticism may be, it does not engage Leibniz or his philosophy, both of which camped in the territory negotiated conversationally in his voluminous correspondence rather than settling in a permanent structure. Hence Deleuze's reading of Leibniz's monadology as a nomadology.

Brown is partly correct in his reading of Leibniz's relationship to More, van Helmont, and Conway; but he is not correct in taking that reading to be a refutation of Merchant. Even in the fragment she cites, it is clear that Leibniz holds More at arm's length. Other fragments make it equally clear that he took van Helmont to be brilliant in flashes but more often merely "paradoxical." In this fragment and others throughout his correspondence, however, there is substantial evidence that Leibniz did not include Conway in the category of "Henry More and his followers" but saw her as a kindred spirit tenting in the very territory he was negotiating philosophically. This does not mark Conway as a source of his philosophy but as a fellow traveler (and, in this minimal sense, an influence), one who shares significant *belles pensées* of the time and articulates them with a clarity that Leibniz apparently thought could help readers (or at least Burnett, to whom the letter was specifically addressed) approach his perspective—a clarity that may still help bring us along.

At the time Leibniz wrote his 1697 letter to Burnett, Plato's work was well-known by way of centuries of extensive commentary filtered through Plotinus and Christianity. Democritus (a contemporary of Socrates) was known by reputation (as he is now), his apparently extensive body of writing having survived only in fragments embedded in the writing of others. Descartes by contrast, who had been dead for less than fifty years, was a controversial and influential figure whose name was synonymous with mechanism and the "new" philosophy. And Henry More, who had died only ten years earlier, was the best known of the Cambridge Platonists and, though an early champion of Descartes in England, was a leading proponent of vitalism in opposition to Cartesian mechanism. Conway (who died in 1679), the limit toward which Leibniz said his philosophical views tended and by which they are here defined, was reasonably well known at the time of writing, though her work in philosophy was even more obscure then than it is now, because it was not published until after her death and was then mistakenly attributed to its editor, van Helmont.[3] The obscurity of her philosophical work alone would make the choice significant, suggesting something unique and indispensable in her philosophical views for defining the territory mapped here by Leibniz. Her inclusion highlights the conspicuous absence of Spinoza. Locke, though not mentioned in the map, is communicated (as already noted) by the context. Conway may have helped Leibniz situate himself for Burnett vis-à-vis those philosophers and the systems they represented. We can be confident that Leibniz knew Conway's work as a result of his extensive contact with van Helmont—both indirectly in van Helmont's conversational references and directly by way of a copy of her *Principles* which he had received from van Helmont. Using her name to evoke a philosophical perspective suggests that he assumed Burnett was also familiar with her work, though it says nothing about what he would have assumed of a wider audience.

The map with which we approach the territory common to Leibniz and Conway, then, is defined by four corners that were clearly marked in the seventeenth century—Democritus, Plato, Descartes, and Henry More (with More being closer to Plato, Descartes closer to Democritus, along the important dimension of vitalism/mechanism)—and by two frontiers— one that divides it from the "empirical" philosophy of Locke, and one that divides it from the "rationalist" philosophy of Spinoza. The philosophical perspectives of Leibniz and Conway (both "rationalist") are "inside," those of Locke (an "empiricist") and Spinoza (a "rationalist") "outside."

Though Aristotle is absent from Leibniz's map, he is the source of much of what we know of the philosophy of Democritus and perhaps

3. The work was written in English but published in Latin translation. Two English translations of the Latin text have become available only within the last twenty years, one by Peter Loptson (1992) and a more modern version by Allison P. Coudert and Taylor Corse (1996).

even more of what Leibniz knew. Reluctant as he was to discuss the "context" of Leibniz's philosophy, Bertrand Russell did note that the framework of Leibniz's formal education was Scholastic and therefore, broadly speaking, "Aristotelian." It is likely that this framework was sufficiently commonplace for Leibniz's generation to make Aristotle's presence as a defining factor go without saying. It is worth noting the successive influences Russell enumerates: Scholasticism (i.e., Aristotle), Materialism (i.e., Democritus), Cartesianism, Spinozism, and, at some unspecified point, Plato's dialogues.[4] This sequence leaves out the early Neoplatonic influence Leibniz himself noted as well as the interaction with van Helmont and, via van Helmont, with Conway's work. This sequence of influences has much in common with the trajectory of Conway's philosophical education, though she had the advantage of being spared much of the formal Scholastic framework that made Aristotle's presence go without saying. Her exposure to Plato was almost entirely of the Cambridge variety associated with More and Cudworth, and her Neoplatonic roots extended to a grounding in mysticism that, though partly shared with Leibniz, was both more deeply personal and more practically political than his.

Aristotle focused on the sciences and their interrelations as well as first principles and their application to motion and material things. He anticipated Leibniz by situating himself between Democritus and Plato: the atomists had relied entirely on material causes and the dialecticians had emphasized formal causes; accurate explanation of things and motion depended also on efficient and final causes. Consideration of causes made it possible for Aristotle to distinguish sciences with distinguishable subject matters, whereas Democritus and Plato practiced a single, unified science. Without reducing knowledge to the motion of material particles (like Democritus) or transforming things into changeless ideas (like Plato), Aristotle derived all knowledge from sensation, tracing steps from sensation to memory to experience (developed from repeated memories) to art and science. The person of experience knows the "fact." Art and science supply the "causes," art for processes of action and production, science for understanding of being and natural change. The "universal," isolated in the recognition of the one in the many in experience, is the basis of the skill of the artist and the knowledge of the scientist. Knowledge depends on discovery of causes and transition from individual things perceived to universals understood—not a transition "from things to constructs or

4. Russell, *Philosophy of Leibniz*, 6.

inventions of the mind," but "from things prior and better known to us to things prior and better known in nature."[5]

Read backwards, this conveys significant insight into the philosophy of Democritus and what it may have meant for Leibniz to evoke his name as a symbol at the end of the seventeenth century. At the time Leibniz wrote, "Democritus" as symbol was shorthand for Leucippus and Democritus and, more broadly, for the "materialist" school that later extended through Epicurus and Lucretius. Consistent with a tradition already well established in Greek thought by the time he wrote, Aristotle assumed that nature (*physis*) was the object of philosophy, which worked its way back from familiar things "to things prior and better known in nature," first things (*archai*). In Aristotle's reading, the philosophy of Democritus and Leucippus included (inadequate) attention to first principles, motion, material things, causes, and knowledge. Causes and knowledge were both understood in material terms, the latter entirely in terms of the motion of material particles. Like Plato, Democritus practiced a unified science identified by method rather than a plural one identified by subject matter.

Reading additional fragments of Presocratic philosophy, including those preserved outside of Aristotle's work, it is evident that Leucippus and Democritus sought to overcome the Eleatic denial of space and motion.[6] In spite of their designation as materialists, they argued that it is necessary for something—space—to exist without being material. Space is a receptacle, a void. Nature consists of space and atoms (literally, indivisibles). Atoms move about in space, and their motion (the "swerve" of Lucretius's *De Rerum Natura*) leads to collisions that result in the objects (divisible aggregates of indivisibles) that we experience. For Democritus, the structure of nature, the problem of knowledge, and the problem of human conduct were closely connected: citations in contemporary and later writers refer to ethics and epistemology as well as physics. Like Plato, Democritus saw these not as separate sciences but as aspects of a unified science applicable to every subject matter.

Locating Plato and Democritus at opposite ends of a spectrum has been conventional since Aristotle. Conventional though it may be, this is interesting in that Socrates—Plato's teacher and the leading character in his dialogues—had much in common with the natural philosophers of

5. McKeon, *Introduction to Aristotle*, xiii–xvii.

6. Freeman, *Ancilla to the Presocratic Philosophers*. Kirk, Raven, and Schofield, *Presocratic Philosophers*.

whom Democritus serves as the final example in Aristotle's account. Not only did this whole sequence of philosopher/scientists share an interest in first things and origins, they also concerned themselves with ways in which "natural" and "moral" orders were connected. Like Democritus, Socrates saw physics, ethics, and epistemology not as different realities but as aspects of a single reality.

It would probably be most accurate to say that both considered that single reality to be natural—and on this point Plato and Aristotle also agreed. The tradition of the natural philosophers that included Democritus derived ethical and epistemological theories from their investigations of nature. Socrates may well have been part of that tradition in that his career followed the same sequence. There is evidence in Plato and elsewhere (particularly associated with accounts of his trial) that Socrates was educated in this tradition and that his earliest work consisted of investigations into natural phenomena. Increasingly, however, his work turned to epistemological and ethical investigations. Plato appears to have started with these investigations and derived his theory of nature from them.

Aristotle opposed Plato's "idealist" approach—which looked at the world and saw forms filled with content—to Democritus's "materialist" approach—which looked at the world and saw content aggregated into forms. What is fundamental in Aristotle's account of Plato is form; what is fundamental in Aristotle's account of Democritus is content. Aristotle's accounts of both were building blocks in the development of his own philosophy, which asserted that "form" without "content" and "content" without "form" are equally nonsensical. Hence the concept of concrete universals.

By placing himself between Democritus and Plato, Leibniz made an Aristotelian move consistent with his Scholastic education but diverging in important ways from Aristotle. In making this move, he chose not to choose sides in the materialist/idealist debate as formulated by Aristotle. And he chose not to choose sides in the mechanist/vitalist debate as formulated in Scholastic/Aristotelian reactions to Descartes.

Not choosing sides is one way to assert that the "sides" have been incorrectly drawn. Defining a territory midway between Democritus and Plato emphasizes not the opposition but the continuum between them. That continuum is marked by shared interest in investigation of a world in which one experiences both wholeness and fragmentation, both motion and rest, both unity and diversity, both form and chaos. Democritus held these experiences together by conceiving a world composed of aggregates of indivisibles. Plato held them together by conceiving an indivisible world composed of aggregates of aggregates. Democritus sought unity at the "bottom" of the world and believed it would be found in parts that could not be divided. Plato sought unity at the "top" of the world and believed it would be found in a whole that could not be transcended. The result in Democritus was necessarily a dual world in which indivisibles and the void were equally real and equally necessary for the existence of the aggregates we experience everyday. The result in Plato was necessarily a single world whose unity would be shattered by the existence of a void or a single thing that was not necessarily part of the whole.

The most fully developed version of Plato's physics is his *Timaeus*, which was also the most widely read of his dialogues throughout the medieval and Scholastic periods in Europe. Here he lays out an "atomic" theory of sorts in that there are identifiable building blocks in the natural world. But it is more certainly a "vitalist" theory in which the whole universe is permeated by soul. There is a soul of the world, and there are souls all the way down. There is no single place in which soul is not fully present. Hence, there is no void: every time and every place is full.

It is interesting to note how fully present Parmenides is at both ends of this continuum—and here in the middle is Zeno, reminding us that the real difficulty is beginning.

Plato addressed that difficulty in a way that is of singular importance for Leibniz and Conway. Some interpreters have reintroduced a sort of dualism at this point in reading Plato's physics, dividing the world between "being" and "becoming." But it is probably more accurate, and certainly more consistent with Leibniz and Conway, to continue to read Plato's world as single by maintaining that "becoming" is "being" encountered. It is not atoms that collide, but souls.

Democritus stands at the end of Aristotle's discussion of the natural philosophers not because he spoke the last word in their conversation but because he is the last thinker so characterized by Aristotle to be included in his discussion. There is good reason to include Socrates in the conversation as a contemporary of Democritus—and to include Plato and Aristotle as their successors. In terms of questions and controversies that drove the conversation, Descartes stands in the same line and occupies a central place in its embodiment since the seventeenth century.

Descartes' "Dedication" to the Dean of the Theological faculty at Paris sets his *Meditation* in the context of a long theological discussion;

but his point is to shift the discussion from "theology" to "philosophy," from "faith" to "reason": "I have always thought that two questions—that of God and that of the soul—are chief among those that ought to be demonstrated by the aid of philosophy rather than of theology."[7] This marks a return to the style of Aristotle's physicists, though it takes up themes (God and the soul) traditionally identified with Plato.

As is well known, Descartes begins with systematic doubt, taking up a gregarious Socratic legacy in a curiously interior way: we can doubt all things, but especially material things. Descartes' point (also Socratic in spirit) is to free us of prejudices and make it difficult to doubt those things that we discover to be true. The mind supposes the nonexistence of all things about whose existence it can have any doubt "and judges that such a supposition is impossible unless the mind exists during that time"[8] The ability to suppose the nonexistence of things about which there can be any doubt requires the existence of mind; the idea of God, which requires God as cause, requires God's existence.

From the time he realized that many of the opinions of his youth were mistaken, Descartes knew that all his opinions and the things built up on them were doubtful. This led him to resolve to tear everything in his life down all the way to the foundations so that he could begin again. Noting that his senses sometimes deceived him, he concluded that he should suspect anything based on sense perception. Noting that the compounding of simple things compounded the possibility of deception, he concluded that those disciplines that concern themselves with "simple" things (arithmetic, geometry) are more reliable than those that concern themselves with composites (physics, astronomy, medicine). In this, he shared Democritus's inclination toward "simples," but not his inclination to look for them in matter.

Having resolved to put aside everything that admitted of any doubt, then go forward until he found either something or nothing of which he could be certain, he wrote: "I will suppose that all I see is false. I will believe that none of those things that my deceitful memory brings before my eyes ever existed. I thus have no senses: body, shape, extension, movement, and place are all figments of my imagination. What then will count as true? Perhaps only this one thing: that nothing is certain." What he

7. Descartes, *Meditations*.
8. Ibid., Synopsis, referring to Meditation Two.

found at the end of this process of systematic doubt was "I," which led him to ask, "But what then am I? A thing that thinks. What is that? A thing that doubts, understands, affirms, denies, wills, refuses, and which also imagines and senses."[9]

Descartes moves from thought or mind (which he takes as more certain) to material things or bodies (which he takes as less certain). Mind (or soul) and God are the most fundamental realities. That I can doubt requires that "I" exist, and that I can think "God" requires that God exist. Descartes ends with confidence in the existence of body, distinguished from mind (or soul) but so closely joined to it that they form one thing. Since he distinguishes mind from body in terms of extension and thought, he ends by claiming the existence of two substances: body, which is characterized by extension, and mind, which is characterized by thought. Naming God and soul as the most fundamental realities places him near Plato on Leibniz's map; but because he separates body from soul, Leibniz places him nearer Democritus and the materialists.

Descartes is neither materialist nor idealist, but mechanist and dualist. Things that have no extension can hardly collide—with each other or with things that do. And that poses a problem in a world where "simple" things are routinely encountered embedded in complexities.

It is a commonplace among interpreters of Henry More that he began with an unquestioned assumption of the unity of reality. Though he was an early and enthusiastic champion of Cartesian philosophy in England, this assumption quickly brought him into conflict with Descartes' dualism. His solution to dualism consisted not in denying the reality of either matter or spirit, but in bringing matter and spirit so close together as to blur the boundary between them. He denied Descartes' exclusive identification of matter with extension, insisting that spirit, too, is extended. Instead, he located the distinction in penetrability: multiple bodies of extended matter cannot occupy the same space at the same time, while spiritual bodies, at once extended and penetrable, can.

In opposition to empiricist epistemology, More, like Descartes, admitted innate ideas, which he defined as an "active sagacity" of the soul, "the mind ordering and systematizing sense-impressions by means of its own original activity."[10] While he denied that ideas such as those of rela-

---

9. Ibid., Meditation Two.

10. MacKinnon, *Philosophical Writings of Henry More*, xxiv.

tion and cause are built up out of externally imposed sense impressions, he did not divorce them entirely from experience. Such ideas emerge in the encounter of the soul's active sagacity with the sense impressions of experience.

Flora Isabel MacKinnon describes More's thought as a tapestry in which numerous threads are interwoven "without too close regard for their mutual harmony." She lists "Aristotle's logic filtered through the theology of the Schoolmen, the mystic pantheism of Plotinus adapted by Augustine to the demands of Christianity, Jewish philosophy and mysticism, the allegorical interpretations of the Cabbalists, the symbolism of Gnostics and Rosicrucians" mingled with "the new science stimulated by Bacon and Descartes."[11] We might add the concept of "deification," which he took up from Greek theological sources at the same time that he was siding theologically with "mystical" and "spiritual" opponents of Calvin in England and on the continent.

Regard for mutual harmony is an apt phrase in discussing More: he was convinced of the harmony of these strands but not terribly concerned about their agreement. This is most evident in his appropriation (or misappropriation) of Robert Boyle's experiments in hydrostatics, which he interpreted as instances of a "Spirit of Nature" derived from the Neoplatonic *anima mundi*. In an important philosophical poem, *Democritus Platonissans*, he depicted an essential harmony between Descartes' mechanical philosophy and his own Neoplatonic mysticism.[12] More objected to "pure" mechanism that rejected all "Immaterial Being," but he was open to a "mixed mechanical philosophy."[13] This openness informed his dispute with Boyle and led to a "monadic" theory in which monads shared many of the physical properties of material atoms.

More and other early modern philosophers grappled with a medieval legacy that Stuart Brown summarizes in four claims which appeared "individually plausible and yet, taken together, . . . *prima facie* incompatible": that God is creator of everything else, that God is wholly incorporeal, that nothing is created out of nothing, and that matter exists. Brown enumerates five kinds of solutions to the problem posed by the incompatibility of these claims: First, an "Aristotelian" solution in which matter is co-eternal

11. Ibid., xxvii.

12. Crocker, "Henry More: A Biographical Essay," 5.

13. Gabbey, "Henry More and the Limits of Mechanism," 26, 27.

with God (which denies the first claim). Second, a Spinozist solution in which God is corporeal (which denies the second claim). Third, a Lockean (and Maimonidean) solution in which God is said to have created the universe *ex nihilo* (which denies the third claim). Fourth, a Berkeleyan solution in which there is only spirit (which denies the fourth claim). And, fifth, solutions such as those of More, Conway, and Leibniz in which all four claims are reconciled with varying degrees of plausibility.[14]

Like Descartes, Locke entered the conversation with Aristotle's physicists by way of epistemology, which he formalized in his *Essay Concerning Human Understanding*, as an inquiry "into the origin, certainty, and extent of human knowledge, together with the grounds and degrees of belief, opinion, and assent" in three steps: inquiry into the origin of ideas (defined as "the object of the understanding" when a person thinks); demonstration of knowledge that results from those ideas; and inquiry into the nature and grounds of faith.[15] Unlike Descartes, he did not believe that there are innate ideas: even if there is universal agreement on some ideas or concepts, it does not prove that they are innate. All ideas come from experience, subdivided into "internal" and "external" sources— observation of external, sensible objects or of the internal processes of our minds. Sensation conveys information about external objects, while reflection conveys information about internal processes.

Ideas may be simple or complex. Human power consists in compounding and dividing simple ideas, which cannot themselves be made or destroyed and which are the basic building blocks of thought. Simple ideas may come into our minds by one sense only or by more than one sense, "from reflection only" or "by all the ways of sensation and reflection."[16] The mind exerts its power over simple ideas by combining them into compounds, thus creating complex ideas; by bringing two ideas (simple or complex) together to view them at the same time, thus creating ideas of relations; and by separating them from other ideas that accompany them in real existence, thus abstracting them and creating general ideas. "Substance" is the substratum wherein simple ideas routinely associated with one another subsist. Locke admits three types of substances—God, finite intelligences, and bodies.

14. Brown, "Leibniz and More's Cabalistic Circle," 90, 91.

15. Locke, *Essay Concerning Human Understanding*, Introduction, 2.

16. Ibid., Book II, III.1.

Knowledge, Locke maintains, concerns ideas alone. All knowledge consists in agreement or disagreement among ideas. This agreement or disagreement may be of four sorts: identity or diversity, relation, co-existence or necessary connection, and real existence. There are three degrees of knowledge—intuitive, demonstrative, and sensitive—and we possess a threefold knowledge of existence: "we have the knowledge of our own existence by intuition; of the existence of God by demonstration; and of other things by sensation."[17]

Locke's inquiry leads him to conclude that the idea is the object of the understanding when a person thinks. Perception of simple ideas is a passion, not an action—but the compounding and dividing of simple ideas (whether in knowledge or in faith) is active and involves will. This is where "physics" intersects ethics: in Locke's account (which at this point has much in common with that of Democritus), "simple" ideas are necessary while "complex" ideas are arbitrary; "freedom," contrasted with "necessity," is associated with will and located in the realm of complex ideas. Complex forms are arbitrary (willed) aggregates of necessary simples. The free person is one who exercises his or her power by participating in the willing of those aggregates.

Spinoza's method (like Descartes') was "geometric": he looked for "given" definitions, postulates, and axioms from which "necessary" propositions could be derived. His *Ethics* begins with seven definitions and seven axioms that plunge him into the heart of the conversation that includes Aristotle's natural philosophers as well as Descartes and Locke. Most significant are the axioms involving cause and effect: because he maintains that nothing is uncaused, Spinoza rejects the idea of contingency altogether. He also maintains that to understand one thing in terms of another is to imply that the two things have something in common. This is important both for his conception of "God" and for discussion of the relationship between human minds and the universe we inhabit. Spinoza argues that there is no substance in the universe except "God." This means that the entire universe is made out of God—that God is the substance of the universe—or that whatever is, is in God. "Nothing in nature," Spinoza argues, "is contingent, but all things are from the necessity of the divine nature determined to exist and to act in a definite way."[18] He distinguishes

17. Ibid., Book IV, IX.2.

18. Spinoza, *Ethics*, Part I, Proposition 29.

Natura naturans (that which is in itself and is conceived through itself—God) from *Natura naturata* (all that follows from the necessity of God's nature). Will, he maintains, "cannot be called a free cause, but only a necessary cause."[19] God does not act from free will: "things could not have been produced by God in any other way or in any other order than is the case."[20] This follows from the fact that all things have necessarily followed from the nature of God. If they could have been different, God's nature also could have been different. If God's nature could have been different, then God could have been different. Since God's existence is "essential," however God "could" be, God "must" be. If God "could" be more than one way, then there must be more than one God—an option that Spinoza dismisses as absurd. A thing is termed "necessary" or "impossible" by reason of its "essence" or its "cause." A thing is termed "contingent" because of the deficiency of our knowledge.

The second part of Spinoza's *Ethics* begins with additional definitions and axioms on which he builds a theory of correspondence between "ideas" and "things." Most interesting is the mutuality of relationship between "mind" and "body" that he lays out: the reality of our bodies depends in some sense on our minds, and the knowledge of our minds depends in turn on the interaction of bodies. The relationship between God and human minds is analogous to the relationship between human minds and human bodies.

Anne Conway left a philosophical notebook[21] and correspondence that reveal a deep acquaintance with the work of Descartes, Hobbes, Spinoza, and More. By the time Conway wrote her notebook, she had joined the Society of Friends, meaning that she had consciously chosen to speak from outside the mainstream of Christian orthodoxy. Nevertheless, she begins, in a thoroughly orthodox manner, with God.

In God there is no time or change, no composition or division. God is "wholly and universally one . . . without any variation or admixture." God is a substance or essence distinct, but not separated or divided from, creatures. This seeming paradox follows from the fact that God is "present in everything most closely and intimately in the highest degree"—though creatures are not "parts" of God nor can they be changed into God (or vice

19. Ibid., Part I, Proposition 29, Scholium.

20. Ibid., Part I, Proposition 33.

21. Published posthumously by van Helmont as *Principles of the Most Ancient and Modern Philosophy.*

versa). Because there is no time or mutability in God, it follows that there can be no new knowledge or will in God. For the same reason, there can be no passion: passion comes from God's creatures, because every passion is temporal, with a beginning and an end in time. Conway maintains that there is in God an idea or a word—the image of God—which in substance or essence is one and the same with God, the source both of God's self-knowledge and God's knowledge of all other things, according to which all things were made; and a spirit or will, of one substance or essence with God, which proceeds from God and by which creatures receive their being and activity. Wisdom and will in God are not substances or beings distinct from God but rather distinct manners or properties of one and the same substance.[22]

Drawing explicitly on Kabbalah, Conway outlines a cosmogony on which the rest of her argument draws: God made creatures with whom to communicate, but the creatures could not bear the greatness of God's light; therefore God diminished that light to make room for the creatures: "a place arose, like an empty circle, a space for worlds." This void was not a mere "privation" (*Non Ens*) but "an actual place of diminished light," the "soul of the Messiah" which filled that whole space. This soul was united with the light of the divinity to make up one subject. This Messiah again diminished its light for the benefit of the creatures, framing the whole series of all creatures. The light of God's (and the Messiah's) divine nature was further communicated to the creatures as objects of contemplation and love, uniting creator and creatures, the source of the creatures' happiness.[23]

Since creatures are entirely a product of God's will, and since God's will is both infinitely powerful and eternal, creation must immediately follow God's will without any interval of time. Creatures are not co-eternal with God (because this would confound eternity with time), but the creatures and the will that created them "are so mutually present, and happen one after another so immediately that nothing can intervene, just as if two circles should immediately touch each other . . ."[24] It follows that there must be infinite intervals of time from the creation, because there is no time so small that it cannot be divided into smaller times. On the one hand, Conway speaks of "an infinite number of times," a "time" that is infinitely divisible (which, as she notes, means any time). On the other

22. Conway, *Principles*, I.2–7, 9,10.

23. Ibid., Annotations to chapter 1, 10,11.

24. Ibid., II.1, 12.

hand, she speaks of the eternity of God, by which she means a being out-side time (with no beginning). Creation, which consists of an infinity of times, is not co-eternal with God, because it is, by definition, in time. The infinity of times also follows from the goodness of God, which cannot be limited. God must have given being to creatures "from everlasting" or else the communicative goodness of God would be temporally limited:

> ... the essential attribute of God is to be the creator. Consequently God was always a creator and will always be a creator, because otherwise [God] would change. Therefore creatures always were and always will be. Moreover the eternity of creatures is nothing other than an infinity of times in which they were and always will be without end. Nevertheless, this infinity of time is not equal to the infinite eternity of God since the divine eternity has no times in it and nothing in it can be said to be past or future, but it is always and wholly present . . .

"Time," she concludes,

> is nothing else but the successive motion or operation of creatures, and if this motion or operation should cease then time itself would cease and the creatures themselves would end with time since the nature of every creature is to be in motion or to have motion, by which means it progresses and grows to its ultimate perfection. And since in God there is no successive motion or operation to-ward further perfection because [God] is absolutely perfect, there are no times in God or [God's] eternity. Furthermore, because there are no parts in God, there are also no times in [God] since all times have their parts and are divisible into infinity . . .[25]

God's will (unlike human will) cannot be "indifferent" or arbitrary. The evil of creatures derives from our changeability, and our changeability derives from the "indifference" of our will. God cannot act without reason. Indifference of will has no place in God, because it is an imperfection. God, though "a most free agent" is also "a most necessary one." God created the world "as quickly as [God] could, for it is the nature of a necessary agent to do as much as he can."[26] Conway argues (for the same reasons that there is an infinity of times) that there is an infinity of worlds or creatures. She notes that "an infinite number of creatures can be contained and exist inside the smallest creatures and . . . these could be bodies and in their own

---

25. Ibid., II.4–6, 13–14.
26. Ibid., III.3, 16.

way mutually impenetrable." It follows that in every creature "there is an infinity of creatures, each of which contains an infinity in itself, and so on to infinity."[27] Anywhere that God is, God, as Creator, must create. There are no "spaces" where God is not, and any place where God is there must be creatures—because where God is, God's creative work is. The continual action of God is one act only, because there can be no succession in God. To the extent that God appears or "terminates" in creatures, God may appear to have succession of parts and therefore time. She explains this with the analogy of a wheel, in which the hub or center moves the whole, even though the center itself remains still and is not moved.[28] If a creature were reduced to its "least parts" (that is to parts that could not be further subdivided) all motion and operation in creatures would cease and it would be as though the creature thus divided were "pure nothingness and utter non-being." She notes that "the division of things is never in terms of the smallest mathematical term but of the smallest physical term. And when concrete matter is so divided that it disperses into physical monads, such as it was in the first state of its formation, then it is ready to resume its activity and become spirit just as happens with our food."[29] She concludes that

> a consideration of the infinite divisibility of everything into always smaller parts is not an inane or useless theory, but of the very greatest use for understanding the causes and reasons of things and for understanding how all creatures from the highest to the lowest are inseparably united one to another by their subtler mediating parts, which come between them and are emanations from one creature to another, through which they can act upon one another at the greatest distance. This is the basis of all sympathy and antipathy which occurs in creatures . . .[30]

With respect to God, all things are made altogether; with respect to creatures, all things are made successively. Conway uses the same dual language to describe Jesus Christ as the essential word and the expressed word.[31] All creatures arise from this "word" and remain in it; but this does not mean that creatures are of the same "nature" as the word: creatures cannot be changed into the word, nor can the word be changed into God.

27. Ibid., III.5, 17.
28. Ibid., III.8, 18.
29. Ibid., III.9, 20.
30. Ibid., III.10, 20.
31. Ibid., IV.2, 21.

We are, she says, children "by adoption." The existence of a "medium" between God and creatures is demonstrable, just as it is demonstrable that there is a God. The demonstration requires, first, consideration of the nature or being of God, and, second, the nature and essence of creatures: the "middle nature," she says, will then discover itself to us immediately. The nature and essence of God must be immutable, because, if there were any mutability in God, it would have to tend toward higher goodness. If there were a higher goodness toward which God could tend, then God would not be the highest good. Creatures, on the other hand, must be changeable: if they weren't, they would be God. The "medium" Conway posits between God and creatures is the "first begotten" of creatures. Conway proposes an "intrinsic presence," which transmits motion with no lapse of time. This enables her to maintain the existence of a "mediator" in the form of Christ while at the same time insisting on the real presence of the creator in the creation. She proposes a two-fold extension, material and virtual, which she describes more precisely as "internal" or "external" motion. Internal motion is essential to the creature moved, whereas external motion is not.

Even more explicitly than her teacher Henry More, Conway rejects the Cartesian separation between body and soul—or "matter" and "spirit"—insisting that they are one substance, not two. She rejects Hobbes (as materialist) and Spinoza (for confusing the Creator with its creatures). She acknowledges a convergence with Hobbes on his claim that all creatures are originally one substance. What she denies, in a comment directed particularly at Spinoza, is that God and creatures are one substance. She joins Hobbes and Descartes in describing extension and impenetrability (which—contra More—she is reluctant to separate), "figurability," and mobility as attributes of matter; to these she adds spirit or life and light, thus identifying herself with a "vitalist" as opposed to a "mechanistic" tradition. Note that "spirit" is an attribute of matter, like "figurability," rather than a separate substance. Loptson discusses this at length. He is inclined to interpret Conway's argument to mean that all matter has something of spirit in it and that all spirit (except God, who is wholly and essentially incorporeal) has something of matter in it. This is justified to the extent that creation is asymmetric in Conway (from God as spirit to matter)—but the more important point is that matter and spirit cannot be entirely separated (as they are in Descartes): there is no "matter" as such and no "spirit," but only animated matter and embodied spirit.

The discussion that follows the orthodox enumeration of God's attributes with which Conway begins addresses a number of significant questions of concern to "rationalist" philosophy in the seventeenth century, but also of importance in the twenty-first: How does "form" emerge out of "formlessness"? How can God be a distinct "substance" while also being fully present to creatures? How are "time" and "eternity" related? How is "change" related to "permanence" or "changelessness"?

Conway's response is not entirely unique: it partly echoes More, partly anticipates Leibniz, and—like much of the seventeenth- and eighteenth-century philosophy that provided a "bridge" to modern science—draws extensively on mysticism, including Kabbalah. She pictures a God that is a trinity of being, word, and will, whose will gives rise through word not only to creatures but also to their being and activity. The cosmogony that she distills from Kabbalah is a rhythm of presence and absence in which the origin of creatures (including the "first begotten") is a withdrawal: creation depends simultaneously (in a "Lutheran" paradox) on God's absolute absence and God's real presence.

Another aspect of real presence is suggested in the immediacy of creatures to God, an immediacy which means that, though creation is not coeternal with God, it consists of an infinity of times. This distinction is an important one for Conway, as for many thinkers in a broadly Augustinian tradition: "eternity" carries a dual meaning that may lead to confusion. On the one hand, it designates infinity of times; in this sense it may be accurately applied to creation. But on the other hand, it designates being outside time, a designation that applies only to God. For Conway, that which has no parts has no time: time is a function of relationship, or of being present to another.

Conway extends Luther's paradoxical understanding of "freedom" in her articulation of the relationship between freedom and necessity: the most free agent (God) is also the most necessary. Evil derives from "indifference" of will, a quality that therefore cannot inhere in God. By the same logic by which she arrives at an infinity of times, Conway arrives at an infinity of worlds: wherever God is, there is God's creative activity. Wherever God's creative activity is, creation is. Since God's creative activity is everywhere, creation is (and hence worlds are) everywhere. It is Conway's discussion of the infinity of creation that leads to her understanding of the unity of all creatures. For Conway, it means that creation (like time) can be infinitely divided: there is no fragment of creation so small that it cannot be divided into a smaller fragment, and so she envisions worlds within worlds within worlds. To reduce a creature to its "least parts" (that is to a point beyond which it can be divided no further) would be to reduce it to nothing, to nonexistence. At bottom is nothing; but one cannot get to the bottom as long as one is "in" the world. Conway's "monads" (like the ones later articulated by Leibniz) are infinite, and they contain an infinity of worlds—all the way "down" and all the way "up." But Conway's monads (unlike those articulated by Leibniz) have windows: the infinity of creatures means that all creatures emanate into one another, suggesting that all relations are internal and immediate.[32] The rhythm of absence and presence included in the real presence of Conway's philosophy means that creatures are present not only to God but also to each other, and that is a social concept of time and space with far-reaching ethical and epistemological implications.

For Conway, as for Leibniz, every portion of matter is a world of creatures containing other worlds of creatures. For Conway, as for Spinoza, God is intimately present in all creatures. Eternity is not infinitely divisible time (which, of course, would be all time). God's eternity is outside time (and—*contra* Spinoza—creation is not co-eternal with God). The infinite is in the finite: the limitlessness of God's goodness means that God must have willed creation "from everlasting." The distinction between the eternity of God and the eternity of creatures means that God must always be fully present in every moment to every moment, whereas creatures may be fully present only across time: God is simply present, creatures are present in time. Creatures cannot be simply present in any moment. No matter where one encounters God, one encounters God whole; but to encounter a creature whole requires time. Thus only God wholly encounters the whole creation. Though creatures are not simply present in any moment, they are whole in every moment and thus, to this extent, "wholly present" to other creatures. But they are also "other" in every moment. The connection of whole to whole within the identity of a creature is analogous to the connection of whole to whole within relations between creatures.

Conway collapses freedom and necessity in God. She maintains that every creature is an infinity of creatures. Infinite divisibility means mutual interpenetration and "intrinsic presence," which is the basis of perception in Conway. Deleuze connects Leibniz's "no windows" formula with the

---

32. Duran, "Anne Viscountess Conway," 64–79.

idea of envelopment: the world is an infinite curve, and the monad represents the autonomy of the inside.[33] Predication is the execution of travel,
but it is not (as in Locke and other empiricists) the imposition of an "outside" world on an "inside" mind. Space/time is transformed into "place" by
dwelling, which requires extension in time and space. Space in Conway and
Leibniz is an infinite envelopment of infinite worlds. Whether perception
is conceived as primarily auditory or visual, space is an envelope around
the perceiver. In visual perception, it is eyes in a body moving through an
ambient optic array that perceive: "it is bodies that think and not minds."[34]
The body is not container, the mind not contained: mind is an extension of
bodies. It is not eyes that see (or brains), but eyes/brains/bodies in optical
space.[35] So the problem is how to describe bodies in space.

This is a point at which Conway proves most helpful. If God is
wholly present in every instant, then God does not take place. Conway's
cosmogony is a movement from singularity, in which all is present in a
dimensionless point (nowhere, nowhen) to worlds, in which all is present
in every point (but "every point" is an infinite set, so "all" is still present
nowhere, nowhen), and "each" is present across a limited set of points.
Beings in process constitute space and make time. Where there are no
beings in process, there is no space and no time. In Conway's reading of
Kabbalah, a withdrawal of light creates space for creatures. She objected to
what she took to be Spinoza's confusion of God and creation, but the incarnation could be read as a claim of absolute identification in which God
"disappears" into creation—"without the world, God would not be God"
(as Hegel put it). Spinoza's pantheism may have confused the two, but
Conway suggested a "panentheism" that by insisting on a God so wholly
present in every point as to be absent absolutely, has a similar effect in
terms of "ethics" and "process."

When Deleuze discusses the baroque, he speaks in terms of "folds"
and a disappearance of "outside." Conway's windows maintain the internal relations important to Leibniz but also open monads to an "outside"
which, as Emerson later intimated,[36] would be everything other than the
monad/perceiver. Of course, the windows also open "in"—but this could

33. Deleuze, *The Fold*, 24.
34. Debray, *Media Manifestos*, 6.
35. Gibson, *Ecological Approach to Visual Perception*, 205.
36. Emerson, "On Nature."

tilt the picture toward Democritus and recreate a world of discrete atoms. Mandelbrot's fractal geometry helps here in conceptualizing infinite "points" in finite spaces, as does Hilbert's discussion of the "actual infinite": a given monad could be finite or limited but still contain an infinity of worlds (in fact, Conway would note, it would have to be). So, each monad is whole, but also related to every other monad (which is also whole).[37]

Russell maintained that every monism is pantheistic, every monadism atheistic.[38] This, he said, explained Leibniz's recoil from Spinoza and his reluctance to articulate a consistent public philosophy. Ironically, Spinoza was accused of atheism by many of his philosophical and theological opponents, though his pantheism rendered the charge absurd. Monism is pantheistic to the extent that it maintains (as Spinoza did) that God is the substance of the universe. Monadism is atheistic to the extent that, like Nietzsche's Zarathustra, it announces the death (not simply the nonexistence) of God. "God is dead" means that God is (always) finished, though there is no end to God. Creatures, on the other hand, are never finished, though we do come to an end.

Where Spinoza recognized one substance, Conway named three: one changeless, one changeable only for the better, and one changeable for better or worse. Think of these as concentric spheres, with the "changeless" encompassing everything. No matter what happens "inside," this sphere will still encompass everything; that which is changeable only for the better encompasses that which is changeable for the worse; that which is changeable for the worse encompasses nothing. The "outer" sphere encompasses time as well as space, and therefore encompasses "possibility" as well as "actuality"—"present" states, "past" states, "future" states, "possible" states. The second sphere is "in" time, as is the inner sphere. (Change for the better in the two inner spheres corresponds to "deification," drawing on some of the same sources as Kabbalah.) This structure is recapitulated in every monad: each part recapitulates the whole, so the whole is not a collection of parts, but a collection of wholes (and each of these is also a collection of wholes). As we have noted, some Presocratic "Greek" thinking conceived of the world as a composite whole made up of indivisible parts (atoms) and so searched for a basic "stuff" at bottom. Conway suggests that the distinctions composite/indivisible, whole/part

37. Mandelbrot, Fractal Geometry. Hilbert, "On the infinite," 367–92.
38. Russell, Leibniz, 172.

be collapsed without abandoning the Presocratic process of division. Divide a whole and you are left not with parts, but with wholes. In this sense, nothing is more "basic" than anything else. Plato and Parmenides began with the One not "at bottom," but "at top." The problem is not how to get a whole out of a bunch of parts, but how to account for the diversity of "wholes" without sacrificing unity.

Perfect freedom would consist in perfect determination—perfect identification of wholes, hence the idea of "conformity to God's will" and the Quaker ideal of simplicity. Sequentially, there is a time and place where/when "simpler" structures exist and more "complex" structures don't—but atemporally (and from the perspective of the whole) all simply exists. Reading back from that perspective (as Plato and Parmenides attempt to do), the "end" may be seen as informing the "beginning" and the "middle." If Plato worked backward from the "end" and Democritus worked forward from the "beginning," Conway worked outward from the middle—and this is the place Leibniz mapped in his comment to Burnett. Since the middle is the one place we can be, it is most assuredly a more secure place to start than the "end" or the "beginning," where we cannot.

7

God and the World

No matter how strong our desire to begin at the beginning, the beginning is always in the middle, where we are: in time, in space, in *this* time, *this* space. Beginning with a backward look, we turn from where we are now toward where we think we began. Not satisfied with beginning, we set out like Descartes to retreat before we begin until we can go no further. But the *now* of where we are and the *then* of where we began are separated by infinitely divisible space: between now and then there is always another then. Like Zeno's arrow, we are suspended in space, motionless. Lost in the struggle to begin, we go nowhere.

If God is in the beginning, we are not where God is, and God is not where we are. God, image of elsewhere, is then. We who are here and now are forsaken by God: this is no pregnant moment, no *kairos*. How can it be expected to give birth?

Confronted with insoluble problems—terrorism, total war, senseless murder—in the middle, in the crossfire, we say that's just the way life is.

This is not new.

In the 1980s, my students in peace studies and ethics classes routinely told me we have to be "realistic" if we are to survive. They would say that we have to learn there are "real" problems such as terrorism (which we didn't call "war") and war (which we didn't call "terrorism"), over which we have no control. These problems were routinely contrasted with "ordinary" problems like getting a degree, getting a job, and making a living over which we do have some control. Being "realistic" meant denying the "real" problems so that it would be possible to deal with the "ordinary" ones.[1]

It was never entirely clear to me whether the "real" problems, like God, were "then" for my students. If so, we were (and are) separated from them by infinitely divisible space: seeking to reach them paralyzes us.

The paradox of this popular theology is that the very act of identifying where we are as "ordinary," manageable, and separated from God leaves where we are entirely at the mercy of the "real" problems. "Here and now" becomes the victim of "then." The image of elsewhere becomes the driving force of ordinary existence. And precisely because they saw ordinary existence as driven, a vast majority of my students clung tenaciously to the American confession of faith: "Everybody's entitled to their own opinion." This is the highest truth of ordinary existence: there is no truth.

As expected, this moment does not give birth. God is neither here nor now. There are only fragments, each with equal validity. The center does not hold. God is dead. On the other hand, it is not so much that there is no truth as that truth is identified with opinion; it is whatever the individual wants it to be; we make God in our own image. Ordinary existence is full of gods identified with tribal and individual truths, all equally valid and equally contingent. The realm of "real" problems is not contingent: it is not full of equally valid alternatives. The god that is "then" is identified with necessity.

The very separation intended to delineate an "ordinary" sphere within which control is possible removes real problems from the realm of human action. Far from eliminating the problems, this separation renders them absolute and subjects ordinary existence to their control. This is another way of saying that they become gods within the realm of ordinary existence. (This seems to have been what Luther had in mind when, in his *Lectures on Galatians*, he distinguished "general" knowledge of God from the concrete knowledge of God in the encounter with Christ, then argued that idolatry has its basis in "general" knowledge of God.[2]) As long as they

1. In the United States, it seems remarkably easy to forget that the problem of "terrorism" and its relationship to "war" did not suddenly appear on September 12, 2001. What we call "war" and what we call "terror" have had a profound impact on our assessment of "ordinary" problems for a long time.

2. In *Martin Luther's Basic Theological Writings*.

are separated from ordinary existence and have no impact on it, one can legitimately claim that they have no real existence. Because they have an impact on ordinary existence (as evidenced by the decision to separate them for the sake of survival), their own existence is secure. They are experienced as *passion*, insulated from human action. They affect ordinary human existence but are unaffected by it. More precisely, they draw their strength from ordinary human existence. Acting as though they are identical with reality gives them the absolute power of reality, the absolute power of necessity.

Human beings are rendered powerless, human history is rendered sterile. God is experienced through the medium of gods that emerge in the "ordinary" human action of separation. This experience of God is an experience of fate: with it may emerge an infinite faith in chance. Everything in ordinary existence is equally contingent and equally valid. What one chooses makes no difference, whether because all options are equally valid or because all options are equally illusory. What one chooses is isolated from one's history; there is no doubt that people act out of character and out of context. Human beings are seen as totally free from constraint within the realm of ordinary existence, because ordinary existence is separated from the constraints of real problems. It is the reality of ordinary existence that is denied.

Without the world God would not be God. Without the emergence of cosmos from chaos by way of possibility, God would not exist. Where God is identified with fate and possibility is reduced to chance, there is no distinction between cosmos and chaos. There is no creation. There is no God, because there is no world. God's death coincides with the death of human action.

This popular theology is a variation on Ivan Karamazov's theme: "If there is no God, then everything is permitted." This theology, unable to conceive of human action that has any connection with the divine, the real, modifies the statement considerably without modifying its functional result: God is not *here*, so everything is permitted. Freedom is experienced as a removal of restraint, a removal accomplished, significantly, by rendering God lifeless, by separating God from life.

Once God is separated from life, the very separation is taken as evidence that there is no God here, that God does not *exist*.

The nature of that evidence is significant for consideration of the existence of God. Simply put, there is nowhere other than here and now to look for evidence of God's existence. At this point the question whether there is a God becomes quite irrelevant, for precisely the reasons suggested by the popular theology already described: an ordinary existence built on opinion and devoid of truth is one in which everything is permitted, and an ordinary existence where everything is permitted is devoid of God.

In *The Cheese and the Worms*, Carlo Ginzburg paints a detailed picture of the cosmos of a sixteenth-century miller known as Menocchio. The picture is entered as evidence that popular culture is not simply a poor reflection of dominant culture. There is a dynamic interaction of "popular" and "dominant" strands, and the popular strand may well convey insights far beyond the boundaries established by dominance, especially the nervous dominance of revolutionary times. It is in that popular strand that one finds evidence of the shape of ordinary existence. My suggestion is that if we explore the shape in the world of the contemporary United States, we find evidence of an ordinary existence separated from God. In Menocchio's world, we find more subtle insights.

Standing before the Inquisitor, Menocchio goes back to the beginning to explain his concept of God: "My opinion is that God was eternal with chaos, but he did not know himself nor was he alive, but later he became aware of himself, and this is what I mean that he was made from chaos." No matter how far back Menocchio goes, he finds chaos and God. The God he finds is emergent, coming into being as self-awareness comes into being: "I believe that it was with God as with the things of this world that proceed from imperfect to perfect, as an infant who while he is in his mother's womb neither understands nor lives, but outside the womb begins to live, and in growing begins to understand. Thus, God was imperfect while he was with the chaos, he neither comprehended nor lived, but later expanding in this chaos he began to live and understand."[3] Mennochio embraces the chaos in which he finds himself immersed; he begins in the middle, and in that beginning he finds evidence of God. The chaos is not an argument against God. It is an expression of human experience, and it stands with God as a description of the reality of the cosmos.

The reality of the cosmos is the first order of business. Menocchio experiences chaos; he assumes God. The challenge is to derive cosmos from those divergent givens. In deriving cosmos, Mennochio offers remarkable insight into the nature of ordinary existence and its connection

---

3. Ginzburg, *Cheese and the Worms*, 55.

to God: "(God) knew all the things that there were to be made, he knew about men, and also that from them others were to be born; but he did not know all those who were to be born, for example, those who tend herds, who know that from these, others will be born, but they do not know specifically all those that will be born. Thus, God saw everything, but he did not see all the particular things that were to come."[4] Knowledge as such, and the nature of the divine intellect, are of secondary interest to Mennochio, though they are of primary interest to the Inquisitor. What is of primary interest to Mennochio is how the creative, chaotic ferment of God and chaos gives rise not only to a living God but also to the world he knows. The Inquisitor's interest in the divine intellect pushes Mennochio toward the insight that general knowledge, total and undifferentiated identification with "all the things that were to be made," *is* chaos. Chaos contains God. God and world emerge in particularity, in separation. Without the world, God would not be God; without God, the world would not be the world.

Chaos is given: God and cosmos are born together.

In spite of Mennochio's unorthodox formulation, this assertion has some orthodox precedent. Thomas Aquinas, for example, is convinced that God's existence is not self-evident. That it is not self-evident pushes Aquinas toward the question of demonstration, suggesting not only a connection between God and the "order" of cosmos, but also a connection between both and the symbols (including language) by means of which demonstration proceeds.

When neuroscientist Roger Sperry pushes as far as he can go, he identifies what he finds in terms different from Mennochio's, but with instructive similarities: "In my own hypothetical brain model, conscious awareness does get representation as a very real causal agent and rates an important place in the causal sequence and chain of control in brain events, in which it appears as an active, operational force . . . To put it very simply, it comes down to the issue of who pushes whom around in the population of causal forces that occupy the cranium."[5]

It is interesting here to keep Aquinas in mind. His five "demonstrations" all revolve around the question of causation, "who pushes whom around" in Sperry's terms, and the possibility of pointing to something

---

4. Ibid., 57.

5. Quoted in Hofstader. *Gödel, Escher, Bach*, 710.

which all people call "God." As before, the "order" of cosmos is important, the connectedness of cause and effect—and for Aquinas as for Aristotle, the primacy of cause over effect, but so is the possibility of common words. Like Anselm, Aquinas places great weight on the possibility of conceiving "God."

Sperry is responding to concerns similar to those voiced by the Inquisitor. Given the appearance of causal forces that leave no room for conscious awareness, it is important to look closely at the emergence of awareness as a causal force. This is as true in the intracranial space Sperry describes as in the all-encompassing space Menocchio described. "If one keeps climbing upward in the chain of command within the brain," Sperry writes, "one finds at the very top those over-all organizational forces and dynamic properties of the large patterns of cerebral excitation that are correlated with mental states or psychic activity . . . Near the apex of this command system in the brain . . . we find ideas."

Sperry sees an unbroken connection between material causal forces and ideas, including awareness: it makes no sense to talk of one without the other. What is most striking about Sperry's images for our purposes is that, while thoroughly immersed in the middle, it is capable of making a beginning toward exploring the emergence of awareness as a causal force. Sperry moves up and down a "chain of command" that includes not only physical interactions on a "low" level, but also interactions of ideas and concepts on a "higher" one. I suspect that the Inquisitor would be as troubled by this image of physical causation as by Menocchio's.

Although Sperry refers to a "chain," it might be more appropriate to refer to a circle. What emerges in Sperry, and in Hofstadter's discussion of Sperry, is an example of cybernetic explanation: what is important is not a unidirectional causal chain, but a pattern characterized by "restraint," a "causal circuit" in which a "nonrandom response" is generated by an apparently "random event."[6] An event at any given point in a circuit effects changes that go around the circuit and reappear at that point in the circuit where the original event occurred, determined by the characteristics of the circuit—and therefore nonrandom. To return to Aquinas, this provides a way in which to speak of causation without positing a "first cause" (though it does require that we posit a "system") and without retreating to an infinite regress. By positing a circular system, it eliminates the temporal sequence that so sharply separates "causes" from "effects."

6. Cf. Bateson, "Cybernetic Explanation," 29–32.

Douglas Hofstadter proposes that we address concerns such as that of the Inquisitor by looking more closely at the concept of free will which he seeks to "unload" by identifying it with choice. To answer the question of whether a particular system has free will, he suggests, is equivalent to asking if the system makes choices. He illuminates this by looking at a number of paradigmatic systems: a marble rolling down a bumpy hill, a pocket calculator finding successive digits in the decimal expansion of the square root of two, a sophisticated computer program for playing chess, a robot in a T-maze, and a human confronting a complex dilemma.

Considering the marble rolling down the hill, Hofstadter assumes (with good reason, I think) that there would be unanimous agreement that the system does not make choices. Even though its path would be very difficult to predict, we do not attribute choice to it, in part because we would agree that, in any given downhill run, it could not have gone otherwise than it did. In the case of the calculator, we would reach a similar conclusion. Hofstadter notes that the argument against choice here would be stronger in a sense, because, if one rolled the marble down the hill a second time, it would take a different path; the calculator, however, would get the same result over and over again. The chess program is a more difficult case. In a program that would execute exactly the same moves under exactly the same conditions, we would be inclined to agree that the situation is analogous to that of the calculator program. As Hofstadter points out, there are programs with randomizing devices that would result in different moves; this is more nearly analogous to the marble. Other programs are capable of learning from mistakes and would not play the same game each time, although memory could be wiped out, in which case the same game would ensue. Of course, the same could be said of human beings: if conditions were *exactly* the same, "choices" would be exactly the same. But conditions are not exactly the same on any two occasions: one cannot, as Heracleitus noted, step in the same stream twice.

Hofstadter goes on to consider the robot in the T-maze. He suggests that we imagine a robot that goes left when the next digit of the square root of two is even and right whenever it is odd. Further, he suggests that the robot be given a modeling capability so that it can "watch itself making choices." If we stopped the robot as it approached the T and asked whether it knew which way it was going, it would say "No." Even though it would be capable of symbolizing the situation (it would "know" the situation, in Mennochio's terms), it would not be described as making choices.

Hofstadter concludes that "unless your mind is *affecting* the outcome, it makes no difference that the symbols are present."[7]

This leads to a further modification. Hofstadter now suggests that we allow the robot's symbols, including its self-symbol, to affect its decisions. "Now," he says, we have "an example of a program running fully under physical law, which seems to get much more deeply at the essence of choices than the previous examples did . . . On a high level we can see the fact that symbols are being used to model the situation and to affect the decision. That radically affects our way of thinking about the program. At this stage, *meaning* has entered this picture—the same kind of meaning we manipulate with our own minds."[8]

Now Hofstadter describes what would happen if someone suggested *left* as the next choice for the robot: "The suggestion will be picked up and channeled into the swirling mass of interacting symbols. There, it will be sucked inexorably into interaction with the self-symbol, like a rowboat being pulled into a whirlpool. This is the vortex of the system, where all levels cross . . . The self-symbol is incapable of monitoring all its internal processes, and so when the actual decision emerges . . . the system will not be able to say where it came from. Unlike a standard chess program, which does not monitor itself and consequently has no idea about where its moves come from, this program does monitor itself and does have ideas about its ideas—but it cannot monitor its own processes in complete detail, and therefore has a sort of *intuitive* sense of its workings, without full understanding. From this balance between self-knowledge and self-ignorance comes the feeling of free will."[9]

Without the *balance*, the experience of free will would be absent: "It is irrelevant whether the system is running deterministically; what makes us call it a 'choice maker' is *whether we can identify with a high-level description of the process which takes place when the program runs.* On a low . . . level, the program looks like any other program; on a high . . . level, qualities such as 'will,' 'intuition,' 'creativity,' and 'consciousness' can emerge."[10]

7. Hofstadter, *Gödel, Escher, Bach*, 712.

8. Ibid., 713.

9. Ibid.

10. Ibid., 713–14.

Does God feel free? This is not a question that would occur to Mennocchio, though it might to the Inquisitor, who did, after all, ask a closely related question about creation: could God have done it all by himself? Confronted with this variation, Mennochio says yes, but not even God can make something without matter. God—like us—is intrinsically connected with matter, and yet God—like us—is described as acting freely. Hofstadter locates that freedom (or its experience) in a combination of self-knowledge and self-ignorance. With Gödel, he insists that self-ignorance is *necessary* in any system, no matter how complete (even a system, we might add, as complete as God). Hofstadter's way of describing this is to say that Truth is more powerful than provability. Mennochio would agree, but he would likely describe it in terms of the co-eternity of God and chaos, the twin birth of God and cosmos. Hofstadter's "Truth" is Mennochio's "chaos" precisely because it *always* engulfs cosmos.

Our concept of God is an undecidable proposition within the system Mennochio identifies as chaos. It might be more accurate to say that God *as such* is the undecidability. As a proposition, the concept exists (as in Anselm's formulation: God is that than which nothing greater can be thought); so does the undecidability.

The concept of chaos is so important because it eliminates some of the problems of temporality and causality that troubled the Inquisitor. Matter does not "cause" God any more or less than it "causes" ideas. Within chaos, both are undifferentiated. There is no before or after, and thus no causal sequence. As in Bateson's description of cybernetic explanation, however, the absence of a causal sequence does not preclude order. The random events of chaos generate nonrandom responses by way of systemic restraints. This is not unlike the treatment that emerges from Augustine's identification of time as "creature"; the question of what God was doing before creation is nonsense because there is no before. With differentiation, both exist: they come into being.

Without the undecidability, there would be only the concept. *Credo quia absurdum.*

Climbing ladders from the physical structure of causation in the human brain to ideas is not the same as climbing from the physical world to God (although the climb is not without precedent—cf. Pseudo Dionysius and Bonaventure). Perhaps that is why Aquinas was so clearly aware that his "proofs" began with God rather than simply ending there. By the same token, climbing down the ladder from a concept of God to the physical world is not the same as demonstrating God's existence. That is why one should read Anselm and Aquinas together: both begin with God. Their "proofs" are more in the nature of icons than demonstrations that compel belief (especially to the extent that icons are understood as a kind of prayer, inspired by the spirit of God lifting up the human spirit).

Along with Anselm and Aquinas, one should add Bonaventure. All three recognized the connectedness of consideration of God's existence, of human knowledge, and of human language. Bonaventure in particular, with his Franciscan heritage, recognized that to know God is to meet Christ and thus to encounter a living being that is not only divine but also human. The key to the question of God's existence is Incarnation, "the eternal in time" as Kierkegaard put it. The eternal in time is the logos, the light by which reason sees. And the logos become flesh is the word of dialogue, of language, and communication.

In earlier discussion of Hofstadter and Sperry, it was suggested that ideas and symbols become causal factors in a system at a high level. Ideas and symbols are not identified with material causes, even though they are clearly linked with matter. Bateson described this in terms of *information*, which he says is of "zero dimension": it is not a thing or an item at all, but a pattern. When the pattern itself becomes a causal factor in the system from which it emerges, we have a situation analogous to the robot Hofstadter described and perhaps the God Menocchio described. Not only is a symbolizing capability present, but also symbols generated are part of the causal system.

In the case of God, Anselm's formulation works well: God is that than which nothing greater can be thought. This identifies God with the Gödelian undecidability that results when the "whole" becomes a causal factor interacting with the "parts" of which it is composed. Obviously, the system is more than its parts, and the concept is not strictly containable: truth is more powerful than provability. As soon as a concept of the whole is generated within the system, the system is transformed. It is now system plus concept of the whole. This works, of course, only if concepts are "real causal agents" as in Sperry's hypothetical brain model. The connectedness between concepts or ideas and matter is, as Mennochio sensed, crucial.

That than which nothing greater can be thought is a "real causal agent." As such, it is constantly transformed, as Hartshorne suggested with his self-surpassing surpasser of all.

The point is that God's existence is the incarnation of language. Or, more precisely, language is the incarnation of God; it is where God exists: "In the beginning was the word, and the word was with God, and the word was God" (John 1:1). It is language and communication, broadly conceived as symbolic form, that brings cosmos out of chaos. God's birth in the word is the birth of cosmos.

From word, world.

PART THREE

Reconstruction

8

Reconstruction: It's About Time

ALEXANDER Boulton connects the centrality of slavery and racism in American history with "paradoxes of the present era" concerned with "the conflicting but equally essential goals of stable political order and progressive reform" and confusion "between the ideals of property rights and human rights."[1] He locates a "parallel" to these paradoxes in Thomas Jefferson: as is well known, the author of the U.S. Declaration of Independence, one of the great documents of international struggle for human rights, owned slaves.[2] Jefferson was a bundle of paradoxes. He was a slave owner. He was an eloquent critic of slavery and the slave trade (as reflected in the draft of the Declaration before it was modified by committee). And he was an early proponent of "scientific racism," a strong voice in the "Enlightenment" tradition from which it originated. This "Jefferson paradox"—or this bundle of paradoxes embodied in Jefferson—is a key to understanding and addressing racism in the United States. In the case of Jefferson, the question is whether the evident flaw of his racism (most obvious in his *Notes on the State of Virginia*) infects and undermines his human rights argument (most notably in the Declaration of Independence). For the United States as a whole, the question is whether

1. Boulton, "American Paradox," 467.
2. Ibid.

113

the racism and racist violence present from the beginning invalidate the American experiment. If the experiment is racist to the core, structural transformation is called for (rather than mid-course corrections or other minor adjustments).

Understanding the "Jefferson paradox" demands careful consideration of the relationship between slavery and race.[3] As Boulton notes, that relationship has been the subject of extended historiographical argument; but, regardless of the position a particular historian takes on temporal precedence, there is widespread agreement that slavery and racial attitudes quickly became so thoroughly entangled as to be mutually defining ideas. There is more controversy surrounding the question of whether racial prejudice is a "natural" phenomenon or a "social construct." Even for those who choose the former and locate racial prejudice in "natural" development, it would be difficult to deny that racism in the United States is a socially constructed and complex interplay of racial prejudice and institutional power and that the "peculiar institution" of slavery played a significant role in that social construction.

Boulton rightly notes that most scholars agree that the connection of "race" with "inherent, biological inferiority" is a relatively recent development.[4] He moves from this observation to the assertion that "the question of which came first, racism or slavery, should be answered unequivocally. Slavery has existed in some form since the very beginnings of complex human society. Race, as either an emotional perception or a scientific category, conversely, can be definitely identified only by the late eighteenth or early nineteenth century, although its roots can be traced back earlier."[5] This is quite right, but it is also potentially confusing. Slavery as an institution is considerably older than modern conceptions of race and pseudo-scientific definitions of race as a biological category. Whether it is older than all conceptions of race is another question, one that is not particularly relevant to this discussion. What is most relevant here, and most critical to understanding racism in the United States, is the interplay of "scientific" racism with the "peculiar institution" of slavery in the United States and the social-political institution of the United States itself. In Jefferson, we encounter one of the primary architects of the political philosophy

3. Ibid., 468.

4. Cf. Marable, "Structural Racism and American Democracy," 6–24. Shipman. *Evolution of Racism.*

5. Boulton, "American Paradox," 468.

and political structures that still govern the United States. At the same time, we encounter a leading exponent of "scientific racism," the author of a "scientific" argument (largely an exercise in "descriptive" science) in support of racial inferiority, who did not abandon that argument when he participated in the institution as a slave owner or when he argued against the slave trade and the institution of slavery itself. Boulton maintains that Jefferson did not see these things as contradictory. In this regard, Jefferson can stand in for the U.S. as a whole: what looks like a simple contradiction (presumably resolvable by rational argument) is more properly a paradox that is impervious to such argument.

Boulton summarizes and critiques Edmund Morgan's "American Paradox" argument, which sees "freedom" as a "reward given to the poorer white planters in Virginia for their support of the planter elite." Morgan sees slavery and freedom as "the contrasting sides of the same coin; without the one, the other could not exist."[6] Freedom, as defined in practice in the United States, "excluded slaves from the social community" and "represented a token advance for lower-class whites in lieu of any real change of situation."[7] Boulton points to "the lack of any direct evidence that might prove the existence of the conspiracy of white planters that Morgan alleges" and contends that "Morgan's thesis seems to rely too heavily on a form of Marxian economic determinism now generally out of favor in academia." Of course, the question is not whether the analysis is "in favor" but rather whether it is accurate. More important is Boulton's criticism of the way in which Morgan's argument is localized to Virginia and the South. To the extent that "New England and the North share none of the moral responsibility for the continuing problems of slavery and race," the argument is seriously flawed. (As Houston Baker Jr. has noted, Malcolm X dismissed this argument by saying that Mississippi is anyplace in the United States south of the Canadian border.[8])

Boulton modifies "Morgan's conclusion that slavery and race joined together early on as a defense of the South's peculiar institution."[9] While he agrees that "ideas of race and slavery did indeed become closely connected conceptually," he also maintains that "there was still space between the ideas to allow considerable confusion throughout the eighteenth and

6. Ibid.
7. Ibid., 468–69.
8. Baker, "Blue Men," 1–12.
9. Boulton, "American Paradox."

nineteenth centuries."[10] Emphasizing the fluidity of the concepts at the time
Jefferson wrote, Boulton notes that "the opposites of Negro and slave for
Godwyn, for example, were English and Christian, not white and free."[11]
Boulton cites numerous eighteenth-century arguments against conflation
of "race" and "slavery," the most interesting being a 1722 Virginia Gazette
comment: "If Negroes are to be Slaves on account of colour, the next step
will be to enslave every mulatto in the kingdom, then all the Portuguese,
next the French, then the brown complexioned English, and so on till there
be only one free man left, which will be the man of the palest complexion
in the three kingdoms."[12] Confusion or no, "America, by the beginning of
the eighteenth century, had become unique in creating a form of slavery
that was dependent upon imagined racial characteristics."[13] Whereas ancient institutions of slavery at least allowed "some permeability . . . some
reason for hope" and did not doubt "the basic humanity of the slave, . . .
by making physical distinctions the identifying mark of the slave," the
peculiar institution of slavery in the United States meant that "emancipa-
tion alone could not end one's servile status."[14] Even more pernicious, as
Boulton notes, is the fact that "this stigma now extended not only through
the course of one's own lifetime but also through all of one's progeny. Both
slavery and race thus supported one another; each became an impermeable character, a fixed status . . ."[15]

Boulton sees this background as constituting the semantic environ-
ment of the Declaration of Independence. At least in part because of the
fluidity of the terms, there is a crucial ambiguity in Jefferson's usage of
"equality," and it is likely "that Jefferson, at least originally, did not at-
tach the same meaning to the idea of equality that most of his admirers
would later associate with it."[16] Many critics have suggested that Jefferson
advocated "only the equality necessary for individuals to compete in the

10. Ibid., 469.

11. Ibid. Notice how this emphasizes national, linguistic, and religious distinctions,
prefiguring distinctions that have returned to prominence in the twenty-first century. It
is a fascinating and important point in assessing documents such as Olaudah Equiano's
account of his life, which is constructed as a "conversion" from African and "pagan" to
European and Anglican.

12. Ibid., 470.

13. Ibid.

14. Ibid.

15. Ibid.

16. Ibid., 471.

marketplace," an equality derivative from property rights rather than a "natural or absolute" equality that is itself a fundamental human right. Boulton only partly agrees with the critics, suggesting that "Jefferson did indeed have a conception of equality based upon natural law," as reflected in his appeal to an "equal creation" derived almost certainly from Locke, in an early draft of the Declaration.[17] Boulton suggests that the very ambiguity of the idea as Jefferson expressed it is one source of its power: "it is an idea that can be used to support almost any position."[18] Not only can be but, in fact, has been.

Boulton reads Jefferson's *Notes* as an "explication" of the Declaration of Independence, a "scientific" grounding for the "philosophical" ideas of the Declaration. Some historians, based on the racist language of the *Notes*, have concluded that, "when Jefferson wrote that 'all men are created equal,' he simply excluded blacks from the category of man."[19]

Some writers have excused the bigotry of the *Notes* as "merely expressions of contemporary opinion in Virginia" and argued of Jefferson that "we should not judge him by our own standards of moral or political correctness."[20] Boulton maintains, though, that, in the *Notes*, Jefferson was participating in "a cosmopolitan discourse on the nature of man and society," not just reflecting local prejudice. This interplay of local prejudice and cosmopolitan discourse is critical. Since even our "cosmopolitan discourse" is limited by constraints of space and time, it is necessarily affected by "local prejudice." In discussions of "rights," that raises questions about the possibility of a "universal" language of human rights as well as local languages that take "universal" rights into account.

Boulton takes Jefferson's antislavery philosophy seriously, documenting his antislavery statements, including his concern with its effect on the white population, and noting Jefferson's "practical success in setting slavery on the course of gradual extinction in the United States." It would have been surprising, Boulton says, if Jefferson had been anything other than antislavery: "As a voracious reader of virtually every important eighteenth-century volume on social, political, and natural philosophy, Jefferson could hardly have been unaffected by the antislavery philosophy that was emerging in the Atlantic world during the latter part of the eigh-

17. Ibid.
18. Ibid., 472.
19. Ibid.
20. Ibid.

teenth century; Jefferson's own philosophy was particularly influenced by the most ardent opponents of slavery: the intellectuals of the Scottish Enlightenment and the French *philosophes*."[21] This is precisely what heightens the paradox. If Jefferson were not antislavery, his ownership of slaves would be unremarkable in the context of a Virginia where most wealthy (and many not-so-wealthy) landowners did the same. It is the philosophical opposition juxtaposed with local practice that brings the case to our attention and makes it relevant to the larger case of the United States. In much the same way that we can inquire into the paradox of an antislavery slave owner, we can inquire into the paradox of a nation that prides itself on its devotion to freedom but does not practice it at home.

Boulton observes that the idea of slavery became associated in the popular mind with the evils of the colonial system at the time of the Revolution, when slavery was used by Washington and Jefferson, among others, as a metaphor for colonial oppression.[22] This metaphor, Boulton writes, was repeated by "virtually every patriot orator."[23] It was precisely this "national language . . . in which slavery and freedom were eternally at war" that drove patriotic slave owners to find another justification for chattel slavery. Hence, race emerged as a justification for slavery in the latter part of the eighteenth century, at the time of the American Revolution. Boulton writes: "The more Americans relied on a philosophy of freedom as a doctrine of rights for each individual to better his or her situation, the more apt they were to use the conception of natural differences to explain the persistent causes of inequality."[24]

"The term 'race' . . . did not acquire its current meaning until well into the nineteenth century. Before then, people belonged to different nations or religions and had different physical characteristics, but all these differences had yet to be catalogued under the scientific abstraction of race."[25] This cataloguing under a "scientific abstraction" proceeded under the influence of Linnaeus and Buffon. The Linnaean species was a "fixed" category. But "where Linnaeus saw stability and harmony, Buffon saw dramatic change and disorder. The world, according to Buffon, was continually in a state of transformation . . . The great biological division

21. Ibid., 475.
22. Ibid.
23. Ibid., 476.
24. Ibid.
25. Ibid.

in the animal kingdom, for Buffon, was between domesticated and un-domesticated animals."[26] Jefferson, Boulton says, would have sided with Buffon—though not with all of Buffon's ideas.[27] For example, Jefferson took issue with Buffon's negative appraisal of American Indians, particularly because Buffon extended this appraisal into an argument for American inferiority.[28] On this issue, Jefferson's *Notes on Virginia* was an extended criticism of Buffon. Though it is a "local" study of a particular state, it is also a comment on the strength and vitality of "America" as a whole.

Jefferson advocated a philosophy of "catastrophism" allied with a philosophy of "polygenesis," separate creations of different races.[29] Polygenetic philosophy repudiated the idea of a single human family with a common ancestor. It thus provided an "out" for the slave owner Jefferson, who could simultaneously hold to the Lockean concept of equal creation and maintain "natural" inequality among human beings. Like many thinkers of his time, Jefferson held to a Linnaean concept of the "fixity of species," treating species as essential categories. He used this in the *Notes* as a basis for his extended argument with Buffon.[30] But it also grounded his understanding of race and led to his support for "antislavery" colonization schemes. Boulton maintains that "Jefferson's comments on blacks in the *Notes on Virginia* should not be read, as they most commonly are, as simply a digression. The underlying subtext that runs through Jefferson's *Notes on Virginia* can be read: the mammoth is a Northern animal whose natural habitat is Europe and America; the mammoth and the elephant are distinctly different animals and occupy similarly distinctly different geographical areas; the Indian and the European are not distinct from one another; the black, therefore, like the elephant who occupies a similar geographical area, is distinct from Europeans and Indians."[31] Though Jefferson urges caution in reaching it, "the whole structure of the *Notes on Virginia* supports the conclusion (inescapable to Jefferson) that blacks represented an inferior race."[32]

26. Ibid., 477.
27. Ibid., 478.
28. Ibid.
29. Ibid., 480.
30. Ibid., 480–81.
31. Ibid., 482.
32. Ibid., 483.

Jefferson's understanding of the relationship between geography and society underwrote his racist conclusions about Africans and Americans of African descent, but it also led to an understanding of the Revolution as a continuation of the struggle between Anglo-Saxons and Normans and a celebration of the "northern" heritage of the United States. Boulton reports that Jefferson went so far as to advocate "honoring Hengist and Horsa by placing them on the Great Seal of the United States. Jefferson praised them as 'Hengist and Horsa, the Saxon chiefs from whom we claim the honor of being descended, and whose political principles and form of government we have assumed.'"[33] He also advocated study of Anglo-Saxon languages at the University of Virginia and sought to establish "linguistic and physical" relationships between Europeans and American Indians.

Boulton describes a "fundamental contradiction" in Jefferson's biological theory, which rests on "the conflicting assumptions of the Linnaean idea of the fixity of species and Buffon's idea of variation, fluidity, and arbitrariness of signs."[34] But he also describes Jefferson's approach as a "grand synthesis of Platonic idealism and pragmatic materialism" that "has been constructed many times in the history of Western thought . . ." A synthesis is a rather different thing than a contradiction. A synthesis that implies a contradiction is a failed synthesis, and I think that is what Boulton has identified in the case of Jefferson and Locke. Boulton notes that "In Jeffersonian natural philosophy, the idea of race plays a role similar to Locke's state of nature; each contains all of the contradictions inherent in the structure of the larger philosophy."[35] Boulton asserts a direct line of development from Jeffersonian science (as a synthesis of Linnaeus and Buffon) to Darwin.[36] It is telling that the critique of this scientific synthesis came from politicians rather than scientists—an indication of the depths of its political implications.

Boulton finds it "paradoxical" that Jeffersonian science made its earliest inroads in the North.[37] But this is only paradoxical if one assumes that the North is less racist than the South, an assumption for which there is no compelling evidence. Southerners tended toward a "theological" justification for slavery and were suspicious of "modern" science. "Progressives" in

33. Ibid.
34. Ibid., 484.
35. Ibid.
36. Ibid.
37. Ibid., 485.

the North could turn to Jeffersonian science for many of the same reasons Jefferson turned to it: it provided a rationale for being both antislavery and racist. As Boulton notes, Northern abolitionists, in most cases, shared the Jeffersonian paradox.[38] More troubling in the long run are Boulton's conclusions regarding the interplay of racial thinking and egalitarian philosophy in the United States. The Constitution, he notes, is an embodiment of the paradox in the form of a compromise, and that compromise is part of the national self-identity of the United States.[39] It has underwritten an "American" inclination toward resolving conflicts without "touching the basic issues of inequality that lay at the heart of conflicts."[40] This leads Boulton to turn to the language of myth, not history of science or political theory. "Rather than directly confronting the contradictions and complexities of the modern age, we have created a narrative that portrays a darker self as a mirror image of our greatest hopes and fears."[41] The conclusion (complete with citation of Claude Levi-Strauss) is appropriately ambiguous, leaving readers to wonder whether the story "deserves to be told" in the language of myth because it has, in fact, functioned as a foundation myth that, true to form, is almost impervious to rational argument—or because the language of myth has the potential to confront the "darker self" (an interesting image with which to conclude an article about race and racism!) that mirrors "our greatest hopes and fears."

It is this contrast between the presumably direct confrontation of rational argument and the indirect approach of myth or story to which I will devote the remainder of this chapter. The contrast raises a critical rhetorical and strategic question for anyone seeking to confront the formidable array of problems related to shifting lines between "us" (whoever "we" may be) and "them" that have already cast a shadow that promises to stretch well into the twenty-first century.

One of the most often overlooked works of nineteenth-century political philosophy in the United States is David Walker's *Appeal*, which takes on Jefferson's argument directly. I mean that in two senses. First, it takes up the structure of Jefferson's argument in the Declaration of Independence, which appeals to a presumably universal court of reason by articulating patterns of abuse that justify violent revolution. Using the same structure,

38. Ibid.
39. Ibid.
40. Ibid., 486.
41. Ibid.

Walker lays out an argument for violent resistance to slavery. Like Jefferson, he speaks to two audiences at once: the international audience of enlightened readers that plays the role of jury in the court of reason and the "local" audience of Americans of African descent enslaved by patterns of injustice that are more than isolated incidents. His rhetoric is revolutionary in exactly the same way that Jefferson's rhetoric is revolutionary. But Walker also takes on Jefferson's argument in another sense, confronting the "scientific" exclusion of blacks from the "human" category. In this sense, Walker's argument uses the rhetorical structure of the Declaration of Independence against the synthesis Jefferson proposes in the *Notes*. The rhetoric of the Declaration itself is not sufficient to counter the racist conclusions of the *Notes*, as is evidenced by the relatively comfortable cohabitation of antislavery sentiment and racism in Jefferson and other "progressives." But the rhetorical structure is another story. Consistent patterns of abuse, sustained across space and/or time, justify revolutionary change. That revolutionary change is simultaneously political (in both Walker's *Appeal* and Jefferson's Declaration) and epistemological. If the structure of our politics is to change in more than superficial ways, the structure of our thinking must change as well. Walker, like Jefferson, has enough faith in reason to believe that a reasoned argument will move a reasonable audience to revolutionary change. But, also like Jefferson, he is willing to resort to arms (and call on others to do the same) where appeals to reason fail. More correctly, both believe that it is necessary (and therefore in accordance with reason) to move to violent means where nonviolent persuasion fails.

This is among the most serious problems that the twentieth century has bequeathed to the twenty-first: the magnitude of violence has grown to levels unimaginable at the time Walker and Jefferson wrote, but violence continues to be treated as a means by which to implement "rational" argument. It is seen in the Declaration of Independence and in Walker's *Appeal* as a logical extension of argument to a new level of power. A similar logic is at work in arguments by "terrorists" (and Jefferson and Walker would have been labeled as such by those in power at the time they wrote) that culminate in suicide bombings, transformation of civilian aircraft into bombs directed at economic targets, and reduction of audiences in crowded theaters to bargaining chips. What is consistent here is an understanding of "reason" that connects it necessarily with coercive power.

Cornel West begins his "Genealogy of Modern Racism" by noting that "the notion that black people are human beings is a relatively new discovery in the modern West." He proposes to give a brief account of "the way in which the idea of white supremacy was constituted as an object of modern discourse in the West." (In light of the aforementioned connection between coercive power and reason, supremacy is the key word here.) West is convinced that "the very structure of modern discourse at its inception produced forms of rationality, scientificity, and objectivity as well as aesthetic and cultural ideals which require the constitution of the idea of white supremacy."[42]

West associates the constitution of the idea of white supremacy with the so-called "Enlightenment" itself. White supremacy and racism are not momentary diversions from or aberrations of the Enlightenment project: they are the "underside" of modern discourse, "a particular logical consequence of the quest for truth and knowledge in the modern West."[43] They are powers within structures of discourse, and they are "subjectless." By this, West means that they are "indirect products of the praxis of human subjects." The point is not to suggest history without a subject, but structures with relative autonomy from the human subjects whose praxis brings them into being. West's focus, unlike that of "vulgar Marxism," is on discursive structures.[44] This is a turn from "rational" argument narrowly defined toward a broader concept of reason that includes other forms of discourse.

West identifies three historical processes that circumscribe the structure of modern discourse in the West: "the scientific revolution, the Cartesian transformation of philosophy, and the classical revival."[45] For West's genealogy, "the scientific revolution is significant because it highlights two fundamental ideas: observation and evidence."[46] He associates it with Galileo's "Platonism" and Newton's "Socinianism,"[47] but also—particularly—with Bacon and Descartes.[48] Descartes, West says, "provided

42. West, "Geneaology of Modern Racism," 47.

43. Ibid., 48.

44. Ibid., 49.

45. Ibid., 50.

46. Ibid., 51.

47. Ibid., 50.

48. Ibid., 51.

the controlling notions of modern discourse: the primacy of the subject and the preeminence of representation."[49] The third historical process, the classical revival, is of particular importance for this inquiry because it "infuses Greek ocular metaphors and classical ideals of beauty, proportion, and moderation into the beginnings of modern discourse."[50]

"The creative fusion of scientific investigation, Cartesian philosophy, Greek ocular metaphors, and classical aesthetic and cultural ideals," West writes, "constitutes the essential elements of modern discourse in the West."[51] This means, he says, that "modern discourse rests upon a conception of truth and knowledge governed by an ideal value-free subject engaged in observing, comparing, ordering, and measuring . . ."[52] It is the "ideal value-free subject" that is most critical for the emergence of modern racism, particularly as it relates to "the recovery of classical antiquity in the modern West." West connects this with the emergence of the "normative gaze."[53] He cites the substantial evidence for "premodern racist viewpoints" but maintains that "what is distinctive about the role of classical aesthetic and cultural norms at the advent of modernity is that they provided an acceptable authority for the idea of white supremacy, an acceptable authority that was closely linked with the major authority on truth and knowledge in the modern world, namely, the institution of science."[54] Of particular importance in this regard is emphasis on visible, physical characteristics as bases for classificatory categories.[55] West traces "race" as a classificatory category based primarily on skin color to Francois Bernier, who, in 1684, "divided humankind into basically four races: Europeans, Africans, Orientals, and Lapps."[56] What West calls "the first authoritative racial division of humankind" occurs in the *Natural System* of Linnaeus (1735), who is responsible for the classificatory system that still dominates the biological sciences.[57] Buffon, too, provided "scientific" justification for racial categorization, and, though he was "a fervent antislavery advocate,"

49. Ibid.
50. Ibid., 53.
51. Ibid.
52. Ibid.
53. Ibid.
54. Ibid., 54.
55. Ibid., 55.
56. Ibid.
57. Ibid.

he viewed black people as essentially inferior to whites.[58] Beyond classification, West identifies a "second stage" in the emergence of modern racism with anthropology and the rise of scientific or pseudoscientific disciplines primarily concerned with physiognomy. Both stages are marked by increased attention to external, physical characteristics as bases for classification and hierarchization. West traces this attention not only to scientific disciplines but also to the arts, particularly via Pieter Camper and Johann Kaspar Lavater. It is critical to be aware of how thoroughly intertwined aesthetic, ethical, and political categories are—and of the degree to which they interpenetrate ostensibly "scientific" ones.

West is particularly concerned to demonstrate the "restrictive powers of modern discourse," which meant that even "progressive antislavery activists" remained "captive to the 'normative gaze.'"[59] He cites Samuel Stanhope Smith and Benjamin Rush as prominent examples, then surveys the uncritical adherence to racist views among Enlightenment authors.[60] For West, it is crucial that "racial differences were justified on cultural grounds in classical antiquity, whereas at the inception of modern discourse, racial differences are often grounded in nature, that is, ontology and later biology."[61] While he concludes that "the emergence of the idea of white supremacy as an object of modern discourse seems contingent, in that there was no iron necessity at work in the complex configuration of metaphors, notions, categories, and norms that produce and promote this idea" and that "there is an accidental character to the discursive emergence of modern racism,"[62] West cautions that "such claims about the contingency of the emergence of the idea of white supremacy in the modern West warrant suspicion."[63] West's point is to avoid reductionist "explanations" of racism while highlighting "the cultural and aesthetic impact of the idea of white supremacy on black people."[64] He goes on to say that "the everyday life of black people is shaped not simply by the exploitative (oligopolistic) capitalist system of production but also by

58. Ibid., 57.
59. Ibid., 59.
60. Ibid., 60–63.
61. Ibid., 64.
62. Ibid.
63. Ibid., 64–65.
64. Ibid., 65.

cultural attitudes and sensibilities, including alienating ideals of beauty."[65] Together, systems of material production and systems of language con- stitute a pervasive system of containment that reaches all the way to the bottom of everyday life.

It is this move to "the bottom of everyday life" that prompts me to take what may appear a surprising turn here, from Cornel West to Flannery O'Connor. I have in mind O'Connor's distinction between "wit- nessing" and "theorizing" in "Some Aspects of the Grotesque in Southern Fiction."[66] Though O'Connor applies the distinction to writers, I think it can be extended to those who are not writers as well. It is an appeal for particular as opposed to synoptic vision: "Today each writer speaks for himself, even though he may not be sure that his work is important enough to justify his doing so." When she says that every writer, in dis- cussing his or her own work, wants to show that s/he is a "realist,"[67] she is making a comment on truth—but also on the extent to which this gets tangled up with representativeness. It is a problem, she says, for writers who don't find the "ordinary" of "great fictional interest," requiring a great deal of explanation (not in the form of theorizing, but of witness- ing). Explanation is demanded even though there are no clear "schools" of American writing, because there is always a critic ready to create one. She extends this to the dilemma of the "southern" writer: "If you are a Southern writer, that label, and all the misconceptions that go with it, is pasted on you at once, and you are left to get it off as best you can."[68] No matter how hard the writer tries to get the label off, though, the general reader assumes that the "southern" writer is "writing about the South" and judges his or her work "by the fidelity" it has "to typical Southern life."[69] She says, "I am always having it pointed out to me that life in Georgia is not at all the way I picture it."

She blames this "realist" inclination on the social sciences, which "have cast a dreary blight on the public approach to fiction."[70] Hawthorne

---

65. Ibid.

66. O'Connor, "Some Aspects of the Grotesque in Southern Fiction," 1961, 36. (Annie Dillard develops a similar understanding of "witness" in her essay "Teaching A Stone To Talk.")

67. O'Connor, "Some Aspects of the Grotesque in Southern Fiction," 37.

68. Ibid.

69. Ibid., 38.

70. Ibid.

may have anticipated this problem when he said he wrote "romances," not "novels," as a way to avoid the standard of orthodoxy established for novels by popular audiences.[71] O'Connor is troubled by this orthodoxy's limitation of the novel to depiction of the "typical": "We have become so flooded with sorry fiction based on unearned liberties, or on the notion that fiction must represent the typical, that in the public mind the deeper kinds of realism are less and less understandable." Works of fiction are not dealt with in their own terms at least in part because the "popular" appropriation of social science makes the "typical" the standard by which all description, including fictional description, is judged. But the writer who resists the "typical," while failing to "partake of a novelistic orthodoxy," challenges the reader to deal with his or her work on its own terms.[72]

O'Connor uses the concept of the "grotesque" to describe the writer's effort to make "alive some experience which we are not accustomed to observe every day, or which the ordinary man may never experience in his ordinary life."[73] The "fictional qualities" of characters in this writing "lean away from typical social patterns, toward mystery and the unexpected," and that is the realism that O'Connor wants to consider.[74] "All novelists," she writes, "are fundamentally seekers and describers of the real . . ." But the particular realism of any author depends on their view "of the ultimate reaches of reality."[75] If "the writer believes that our life is and will remain essentially mysterious," then a "realistic" fiction "will always be pushing its own limits outward toward the limits of mystery."[76] The writer "will be interested in what we don't understand rather than what we do."[77] (John Cage made much the same point in reference to his music.) But the writer who is interested in mystery cannot "slight the concrete": "Fiction begins where human knowledge begins—with the senses—and every fiction writer is bound by this fundamental aspect of his medium."[78] The writer

71. Ibid.
72. Ibid., 39.
73. Ibid., 40.
74. Ibid.
75. Ibid., 40–41.
76. Ibid., 41.
77. Ibid.
78. Ibid., 42.

of "grotesque fiction," O'Connor says, is always "looking for one image to connect two points, one concrete, one invisible," both equally real.[79]

The look of this fiction, she says, is going to be "wild": "it is almost of necessity going to be violent and comic, because of the discrepancies it seeks to combine."[80] O'Connor comments that "it's considered an absolute necessity these days for writers to have compassion," but she is skeptical of this if it means (as it often does) that "the writer excuses all human weakness because human weakness is human." But she wants to maintain the writer's critical edge, the capacity to be "anti": "Certainly when the grotesque is used in a legitimate way, the intellectual and moral judgments implicit in it will have the ascendancy over feeling."[81]

"In the novelist's case," O'Connor writes, "prophecy is a matter of seeing near things with their extensions of meaning and thus of seeing far things close up. The prophet is a realist of distances, and it is this kind of realism that you find in the best modern instances of the grotesque."[82] She maintains that the South still has a "theological" conception of the human—implying with the "still" that others (the North?) once had this but have now lost it. More specifically, she seems to mean "Christian"— but in a sense that is not entirely orthodox. She comes to this claim via a comment on writing about "freaks": "Whenever I'm asked why Southern writers particularly have a penchant for writing about freaks, I say it is because we are still able to recognize one . . . . while the south is hardly Christ-centered, it is most certainly Christ-haunted."[83] It is a "ghost," then, that provides the measure against which the "normal" and the "grotesque" are judged in Southern literature; and "ghosts," O'Connor says, "can be very fierce and instructive."

She carries this a step further by suggesting that the Southern writer is "haunted" by more than "Christ."[84] Such a writer is equally haunted by other Southern writers, one in particular: "The presence alone of Faulkner in our midst makes a great difference in what the writer can and cannot permit himself to do. Nobody wants his mule and wagon stalled on the

79. Ibid.
80. Ibid., 43.
81. Ibid.
82. Ibid., 44.
83. Ibid.
84. Ibid., 45.

same track the Dixie Limited is roaring down." The multiple hauntings mean that "the Southern writer is forced on all sides to make his gaze extend beyond the surface, beyond mere problems, until it touches that realm which is the concern of prophets and poets."[85]

Here, she returns to Hawthorne's claim to be writing "romances" rather than novels, a claim she sees as an attempt "to keep for fiction some of its freedom from social determinisms, and to steer it in the direction of poetry."[86] By this, O'Connor seems to have in mind the task of seeing through existing conditions into the depths, as it were. (Samuel Taylor Coleridge made a similar claim for the task of the poet in *Biographia Literaria*.) In response to critics who want a surface realism (as opposed to the deep realism she is describing), O'Connor says that "a literature which mirrors society would be no fit guide for it."[87] She writes that "in the name of social order, liberal thought, and sometimes even Christianity, the novelist is asked to be the handmaid of his age."[88] But the novelist is unfit for the function of "domestic"—given that function, s/he "is going to set the public's luggage down in puddle after puddle."[89]

It is not the novelist's function, though, but the novelist's "vision" that is critical for O'Connor. Writers "who speak for and with their age are able to do so with a great deal more ease and grace than those who speak counter to prevailing attitudes."[90] O'Connor tells the story of a letter she received from "an old lady in California" who informed her "that when the tired reader comes home at night, he wishes to read something that will lift up his heart. And it seems her heart had not been lifted up by anything of mine she had read. I think that if her heart had been in the right place, it would have been lifted up."[91] O'Connor's critical response categorizes this reader as less than "serious." Speaking directly to her audience, O'Connor says, "You may say that the serious writer doesn't have to bother about the tired reader, but he does, because they are all tired."[92] The response of the "ordinary" reader is indicative of the demand for "the redemptive

85. Ibid.
86. Ibid., 45–46.
87. Ibid., 46.
88. Ibid.
89. Ibid., 47.
90. Ibid.
91. Ibid., 47–48.
92. Ibid., 48.

act."[93] O'Connor's response is to accept the demand while noting that the "common reader" has forgotten the cost of redemption. It does not come cheap or easy.

In a world that is off-balance, novelists cannot reflect balance but must "achieve one from a felt balance inside" themselves.[94] This means that "the great novels we get in the future are not going to be those that the public thinks it wants, or those that critics demand" and that "the direction of many of us will be more toward poetry than toward the traditional novel." The image she presents, against the "old lady in California" who wants her heart "lifted up," is of "a descent through the darkness of the familiar into a world where, like the blind man cured in the gospels, he sees men as if they were trees, but walking. This is the beginning of vision," and it is vision that O'Connor is interested in. She concludes: "I hate to think that in twenty years Southern writers too may be writing about men in gray-flannel suits and may have lost their ability to see that these gentlemen are even greater freaks than what we are writing about now. I hate to think of the day when the Southern writer will satisfy the tired reader."[95]

I think it is important to point out here that O'Connor does not neglect the tired reader. (Remember, she said we're all tired!) Rather, she resists the claim that the novelist's task is to "satisfy" that reader. In this regard, I recall that Rosa Parks explained her refusal to surrender her seat to a white rider on a Montgomery, Alabama, bus by saying she was "tired." Some people have mistakenly interpreted that as evidence of an "apolitical" motivation, but the "tired" reader who is not satisfied may be precisely the one who remembers the cost of redemption.

Alice Walker is one of those readers.

In "Beyond the Peacock," she reports that she was reminded after a poetry reading "at a recently desegregated college in Georgia" that she and Flannery O'Connor had lived within minutes of each other in 1952.[96] Even though Walker was only eight at the time (twenty years younger than O'Connor) and she and her family moved away after less than a year, she found the coincidence intriguing, and it set her to thinking again about O'Connor and her work.

93. Ibid.
94. Ibid., 49.
95. Ibid., 50.
96. Walker, "Beyond the Peacock," 42.

She says that she read O'Connor "endlessly" in college, put her away in anger while she "searched for, found, and studied black women writers,"[97] but took her up again because she could "never be satisfied with a segregated literature."[98]

Walker describes a 1974 journey with her mother to visit the two old houses—the one where she lived and the one where Flannery O'Connor lived. She speaks of "revisiting the past," but it is "peacocks and abandoned houses" rather than literature and writers that pique her mother's curiosity.[99]

The first thing they encounter is "a fence, a gate, a NO TRESPASSING sign"—and the shock of remembering that they lived "in a pasture." Walker hesitates, but her mother has already opened the gate: "To her, life has no fences, except, perhaps, religious ones, and these we have decided not to discuss."[100] Her mother is present to the past, daring the landlord to say anything about "trespassing," recalling that he still owes her for a crop, that he never gave her her half of the calves she raised that year. She still refers to the daffodils (which are still there) as "my daffodils."[101] Alice Walker emphasizes the contrasting memories that she and her mother experience as they stand in the same place facing the same scene but seeing very different things.

Walker notes that "there is a garish new Holiday Inn directly across Highway 441 from Flannery O'Connor's house," a tribute to the interweaving of memory with tourism, of memory and its commodification.[102] The discussion between Walker and her mother is telling; the topics are "O'Connor, integration, the inferiority of the corn muffins we are nibbling, and the care and raising of peacocks."[103] It turns to the question of why Alice Walker likes Flannery O'Connor. Her mother responds to Walker's comment that O'Connor was "a Catholic . . . which must not have been comfortable in the Primitive Baptist South, and more than any other writer she believed in everything, including things she couldn't see"

97. Ibid., 42.
98. Ibid., 43.
99. Ibid.
100. Ibid.
101. Ibid., 44.
102. Ibid., 45.
103. Ibid., 45–46.

by asking, "Is that why you like her?" Walker responds, "I like her because she could write."[104]

Walker's short biography of O'Connor locates her vis-à-vis slavery: the house she lived in with her mother in Milledgeville "was built by slaves who made the bricks by hand."[105] Her biographers, Walker says, "are always impressed by this fact, as if it adds the blessed sign of aristocracy, but whenever I read it I think that those slaves were some of my own relatives, toiling in the stifling, middle-Georgia heat, to erect her grandfather's house, sweating and suffering the swarming mosquitoes as the house rose slowly, brick by brick." She says she always stands in the backyard when she visits "antebellum homes in the South . . . gazing up at the windows," then goes inside to stand at the windows "looking down into the backyard." It is, she says, "between the me that is on the ground and the me that is at the windows" that "History is caught."[106]

Walker continues the biography through the onset of lupus, which she describes in some detail: "It is a painful, wasting disease, and O'Connor suffered not only from the disease—which caused her muscles to weaken and her body to swell, among other things—but from the medicine she was given to fight the disease, which caused her hair to fall out and her hipbones to melt."[107]

This reflection is followed by her mother's question—what are you looking for when you make these trips back to the South?[108] Walker's response is "a wholeness," which she elaborates by talking about an exchange before she spoke to a gathering of Mississippi librarians: "one of the authorities on Mississippi history and literature got up and said she really did think Southerners wrote so well because 'we' lost the war. She was white, of course, but half the librarians in the room were black."[109] Alice Walker got up and said, "no, 'we' didn't lose the war. 'You all' lost the war. And you all's loss is our gain."[110] Walker describes the work of the writer as being to write "the missing parts to the other writer's story." "The

---

104. Ibid., 46.
105. Ibid., 46–47.
106. Ibid., 47.
107. Ibid., 48.
108. Ibid.
109. Ibid., 49.
110. Ibid.

whole story," she says, is what she's after—to which her mother responds, "Well, I doubt if you can ever get the true missing parts of anything away from the white folks . . . they've sat on the truth so long by now they've mashed the life out of it."[111]

Walker relates the story of *Everything That Rises Must Converge* to her mother.[112] A "middle-aged" white woman "gets on a bus with her son, who likes to think he is a Southern liberal . . . he looks for a black person to sit next to. This horrifies his mother, who, though not old, has old ways. She is wearing a very hideous, very expensive hat, which is purple and green." In the conversation with her mother, Walker builds up just how expensive the hat is and how it was bought "at the best store in town." A "large black woman, whom O'Connor describes as looking something like a gorilla, gets on the bus with a little boy, and she is wearing this same green-and-purple hat."[113] The "white lady," of course is "horrified, outdone." O'Connor, Walker explains to her mother, thought the South would become just like the North. In response to her mother's question, Walker agrees that this will happen but goes on with the story. When they get off the bus, the white woman offers the little boy (with whom she has been "flirting") a "bright new penny," and the boy's mother "knocks the hell out of her with her pocketbook." Hearing the story, Walker's mother sympathetically says "'Poor thing' . . . in a total identification that is so Southern and so black."[114] Though O'Connor didn't say what the black woman did after she walked away, Walker tells her mother that she might know "the other half" of the story.[115] Part of the power of the story for Walker is that it moves into its audience to be completed.[116]

Walker writes that she discovered O'Connor in college in the North when she took a course in "Southern writers and the South."[117] She says that "the perfection" of O'Connor's writing was "so dazzling" that she didn't notice "that no black Southern writers were taught."[118] Walker says that she first appreciated O'Connor for her depiction of Southern white women—

111. Ibid.
112. Ibid.
113. Ibid., 50.
114. Ibid., 51.
115. Ibid.
116. On this point, cf. Paul Ricoeur's analysis in *Time and Narrative*.
117. Walker, "Beyond the Peacock," 51.
118. Ibid., 51.

without "a whiff of magnolia."[119] Walker appreciates the distance O'Connor maintains in her description of black characters as "a kind of grace many writers do not have when dealing with representatives of an oppressed people within a story." O'Connor "leaves them free, in the reader's imagination, to inhabit another landscape, another life, than the one she creates for them." She does not insist on "knowing everything," on "being God."[120]

This is not to deny O'Connor's racism, but, Walker writes, "essential O'Connor is not about race at all."[121] Walker writes about the transformation of black characters from passive to active in O'Connor's first published short story "The Geranium," which became "Judgment Day" in its final version. "The quality added," Walker writes, "is rage, and, in this instance, O'Connor waited until she saw it exhibited by black people before she recorded it."[122]

O'Connor's house, called Andalusia, is, of course, well cared for. Walker writes, "what I feel at the moment of knocking is fury that someone is paid to take care of her house, though no one lives in it, and that her house still, in fact, stands, while mine—which of course we never owned anyway—is slowly rotting into dust. Her house becomes—in an instant— the symbol of my own disinheritance, and for that instant I hate her guts. All that she has meant to me is diminished, though her diminishment within me is against my will."[123]

Walker writes,

> My bitterness comes from a deeper source than my knowledge of the difference, historically, race has made in the lives of white and black artists. The fact that in Mississippi no one even remembers where Richard Wright lived, while Faulkner's house is maintained by a black caretaker is painful, but not unbearable. What comes close to being unbearable is that I know how damaging to my own psyche such injustice is. In an unjust society the soul of the sensitive person is in danger of deformity from just such weights as this. For a long time I will feel Faulkner's house, O'Connor's house, crushing me. To fight back will require a certain amount of energy, energy better used doing something else.[124]

119. Ibid., 52.
120. Ibid.
121. Ibid., 53.
122. Ibid., 54.
123. Ibid., 57.
124. Ibid., 58.

Walker's conclusion returns to the peacocks of the title and of her earlier discussion with her mother:

> As we leave O'Connor's yard the peacocks—who she said would have the last word—lift their splendid tails for our edification. One peacock is so involved in the presentation of his masterpiece he does not allow us to move the car until he finishes with his show.
>
> "Peacocks are inspiring," I say to my mother, who does not seem at all in awe of them and actually frowns when she sees them strut, "but they sure don't stop to consider they might be standing in your way."
>
> And she says, "Yes, and they'll eat up every bloom you have, if you don't watch out."[125]

In "The Site of Memory," a lecture Toni Morrison delivered while she was working on *Beloved*, Morrison writes first of the relationship between memoir and fiction and traces the tradition of memoir in the United States to slave narratives.[126] Writing of these narratives, she says that "As determined as these black writers were to persuade the reader of the evil of slavery, they also complimented him by assuming his nobility of heart and his high-mindedness."[127] Literacy, she writes, was power. "No slave society in the history of the world," she continues, "wrote more—or more thoughtfully— about its own enslavement."[128] These writers, she says, pull the narrative up short repeatedly. As a writer of fiction, Morrison says she is more interested than the writers of slave narratives in interior life. She is interested in how to rip away the veil that has often been discretely placed over terrible memories. She describes this in almost religious terms: "If writing is thinking and discovery and selection and order and meaning, it is also awe and reverence and mystery and magic." She addresses the distinction often made between fiction and fact. Fiction, she is convinced, is deeply concerned with truth: the proper distinction is not fact/fiction but fact/truth.

Morrison returns to her childhood, and she pays careful attention to the process of memory as it is related to the stories one remembers (and

125. Ibid., 59.
126. Morrison, "Site of Memory," 299.
127. Ibid., 300.
128. Ibid., 301.

tells). In her own writing, Morrison says, "the image comes first and tells me what the 'memory' is about"[129]

"Authors arrive at text and subtext in thousands of ways," she writes, "learning each time they begin anew how to recognize a valuable idea and how to render the texture that accompanies, reveals or displays it to its best advantage. . . . You know," she continues, "they straightened out the Mississippi River in places, to make room for houses and livable acreage. Occasionally the river floods these places. 'Floods' is the word they use, but in fact it is not flooding; it is remembering. Remembering where it used to be. All water has a perfect memory and is forever trying to get back to where it was. Writers are like that: remembering where we were, what valley we ran through, what the banks were like, the light that was there and the route back to our original place. It is emotional memory— what the nerves and the skin remember as well as how it appeared. And a rush of imagination is our 'flooding.' . . . Like water," she concludes, "I remember where I was before I was 'straightened out.'"[130]

I began this chapter with the "reasoned" argument of an antislavery advocate, Thomas Jefferson, who owned slaves and contributed significantly to a racist argument that made it possible for him—and Americans who followed him—to live with that. I turned, then, to a reasoned argument in response, that of David Walker. Walker shared Jefferson's faith in reason in that he believed he could talk Jeffersonian racists out of racism or, failing that, inspire its victims to "rational" violence—violence within the limits of reason—to end it. But I end with something much more akin to myth, the place of memory. Antiracist visions, like visions of peace, are often dismissed as "unrealistic," but Alice Walker's Flannery O'Connor, Walker herself, and Toni Morrison give me reason to hope that those visions are realisms of distance. Telling the present story with honesty, humility, and humor may give us the distance-vision we need to see into the depths, where our myths lie, largely unnoticed. That may, at least, enable us to resist being "straightened out" and get our hearts in the right place to be lifted.

129. Ibid., 303.
130. Ibid., 305.

9

The Shape of the City

I T is instructive that the most influential philosophy of nonviolence articulated in the twentieth century begins with an epistemological claim and an explicit reference to a principled political statement from the previous century, while it sinks its roots through two concrete political struggles into ancient texts from two distinct religious traditions. Gandhi defines *satyagraha* as holding on to truth, thereby associating it simultaneously with knowing and with doing—not only speaking truth to power, as the old Quaker expression would have it, but joining truth with power in a philosophy of action. This philosophy betrays Socratic roots (and goes against the grain of professional philosophy in the twentieth century) by demanding passionate holding on rather than dispassionate knowing. Gandhi began to develop this philosophy in a community of resistance to oppression in South Africa, a genealogical note that directs our attention to *satyagraha's* sister, the struggle against apartheid that developed into the African National Congress, born in the same time and place as the Gandhian philosophy that guided India's independence struggle. Gandhi's explicit reference to Thoreau's "Civil Disobedience" adds an important dimension: a common ancestor shared by these twins born in the early twentieth century is the nineteenth-century struggle against slavery, particularly that portion of the struggle which insisted that a slave state by definition had sacrificed its legitimacy as a state (and reminded the northern states of the United States that every state was a slave state as long as slavery was sanctioned in any state of the union). Gandhi's reference to Thoreau evokes a political philosophy that is critical for the practice of nonviolence, particularly as it develops near the end of the twentieth century in a series of "velvet" revolutions, from the Philippines to the Czech Republic and the former Soviet Union: all government derives its power (as well as its authority) from the consent of the governed. Like Thoreau, Gandhi insists that this political claim translates directly into an ethical imperative that is also a descriptive statement about the nature of reality, a metaphysical claim: every individual act is a proclamation of the type of city in which we consent to live and a contribution to the building of that city (as in the parallel *polis* of Václav Havel and Charter 77). No act is innocent, no act is isolated, no act is disconnected.

This recognition is a reminder to expand our genealogy in two dimensions, to a feminist movement that Gandhi recognized (though not in an entirely positive way) as a cousin, and to the philosophy of Martin Luther King Jr., which King located in his encounter with Gandhi and Thoreau as well as his much earlier encounter with the gospel of Christianity. If *satyagraha* as embodied in the Indian independence movement is the twin sister of the struggle against apartheid as embodied in the African National Congress, then both are descendants of the struggle against slavery and the struggle for the rights of women (also twins, as Sarah Grimké, Angelina Grimké, and Frederick Douglass were aware)—and the Civil Rights movement in the United States is their younger sibling. The struggle for the rights of women in particular came to insist that the personal is political, and Martin Luther King Jr.'s embrace of the personalist tradition in which he was immersed at Boston University meant that this would echo also through the Civil Rights movement.

Gandhi's explicit epistemological claim is that, because all human knowing is incomplete, we can never have a sufficient basis on which to ground violent action. Violence, quite simply, can never be justified in a human context. This is not to say that violence never occurs but rather that when it does occur it is a failure, a denial of humanity. Violence makes a claim about our knowing that we cannot sustain, and Gandhi sees that, first and foremost, as a denial of truth. His response is to insist on a passionate holding on to truth that refuses violence in every instance. This passionate holding on, he argued, can result in harm to the one doing the holding—but it does not inflict harm on others. (Hence his invocation of the concept of *ahimsa*, non-harm, which he shares with the Jain tradition.) While acknowledging Thoreau, Gandhi distinguishes *satyagraha* from civil disobedience. As he understands it, the emphasis in civil disobedience is on its civility more than its disobedience. As noted above, every individual act of every individual is both a proclamation of the type of city one consents to inhabit and a contribution to its construction. In that sense, every act may be understood as "civil" and "political." A specific act of disobedience (such as Thoreau's refusal to pay taxes) is civil in this sense, but it is also a calculated contribution to the dismantlement of a government that is no longer deemed legitimate by the one engaged in disobedience. Gandhi's *satyagraha* is intended to guide everyday civil action and inform specific acts of disobedience, but it is not identified with those acts of disobedience. Gandhi also distinguishes *satyagraha* from the passive resistance he identifies with advocates of women's suffrage. *Satyagraha*, he argues, is not passive and must not be undertaken from a position of weakness. For Gandhi, *satyagraha* is active (though it is an appropriately paradoxical act of seizing the passionate holding on to truth, reminiscent of the action in inaction, inaction in action of the *Bhagavadgita*), and it is not an interim measure dictated by inability to impose one's will by violent means. This is an important point to which we will return, both because it introduces a potential misunderstanding of the struggle for women's rights and because it raises the question of power as it relates to the practice of nonviolence. Gandhi's political philosophy depends on the claim that the power of government derives from the consent of the governed. If that is an accurate claim, then the consent of the governed (in both passive and active forms) is the most critical dimension of political philosophy, and the power of the powerless is not to be underestimated. There is a democratic imperative here that cannot be disentangled from the family to which Gandhian nonviolence belongs.

With Thoreau, anarchism enters the family tree. Recall that he begins "Civil Disobedience" by affirming the proposition that "That government is best which governs least," asserting that, in the end, this comes to "That government is best which governs not at all." This is another way of saying that power is in the hands of the governed. Because it insists that this power is in the hands of each and every one of the governed (rather than in a collective mass, whether the whole or the majority or a revolutionary vanguard), it is easily distorted in a milieu permeated by individualism.

In the hands of Gandhi as in the hands of Thoreau, it is nothing less than an imperative for principled individual action as the constituent unit of social justice. This is critical. Thoreau distinguishes a universe turned in such a way as to derive (individual) power from an external source from one turned in such a way as to locate power originally in an internal source. This has strategic significance, for example, when the question of petitioning authority arises. To petition government for rights is to imply that those rights are the government's to give. Both Thoreau and Gandhi criticize such action as a distortion of truth, though neither denies the symbolic power of petitions as educational devices—both because of their potential to shame individual members of a government that has acted unjustly and because of their potential to bring masses of people to awareness of rights of which they were previously unaware. Petition campaigns in the United States, India, and South Africa have performed both of these functions at important historical moments, particularly when their symbolic character has been made clear. The danger of distortion resides in confusion of principled individual action with action motivated by self-interest. The distinction is a subtle one, and I am convinced that it lies at the heart of a great deal of confusion in political philosophy—particularly variations on classical liberalism that have tended toward simple utilitarianism in the service of free markets rather than free human beings. Note that power in Thoreau and Gandhi consists in a relationship between the individual (whose knowing is always necessarily partial) and Truth. Gandhi makes this most explicit in *satyagraha*: power consists in the passionate holding on, not in the interest, of the individual. As Gandhi noted, this does not guarantee that the individual who passionately holds on to truth will always be correct (the necessarily partial character of all our knowing weighs heavily against this). And, in fact, the necessarily partial character of our knowing is critical to a practice of *satyagraha* that will contribute to a just civil society. Recognition of that partial character is what impels the individual not only to passionately hold on to truth but also to refuse to violently impose that truth on others. Passionate holding on to truth without a renunciation of violence tends toward final solutions. Those against whom such solutions have been directed are in a position to see this with greater clarity than those who have directed them or simply acquiesced in them, and this suggests that all who hold on passionately to truth must listen with care, even across barriers that appear impermeable. Thoreau's argument is that when all individual human beings combine this passionate holding on to truth with openness to others, government will not be necessary. Government is not a source of power so much as an expedient, a temporary means, by which to curb abuse of power and diminish the destructive potential of human weakness. (Note that, in this view, it is government, not nonviolent action, that is an interim measure, a temporary expedient.) For Thoreau, the point is not to hold on to law but to hold on to truth. This is particularly important as a foundation for resistance in situations where law is on the side of oppression (as in Nazi Germany, apartheid South Africa, Jim Crow United States, etc.). Thoreau is willing to acknowledge that law can be a useful thing, but he is not willing to acknowledge that respect for law as such should be cultivated as part of what it means to be a citizen. Respect for law as such lays a foundation for blind obedience that has been increasingly destructive in the century and a half since Thoreau wrote. What is to be respected is right, and that may mean breaking the law. This was taken up by Gandhi and the Indian resistance and articulated in Martin Luther King Jr.'s elaboration of Augustine: an unjust law is no law.

King's adoption of Gandhi's translation of *satyagraha* as "truth-force" and his equation of "truth" with "love" are important developments of the philosophy of nonviolence associated with Gandhi (note that Gandhi linked it to "soul," calling it "soul-force" as well as "truth-force"). In the tradition of Greek philosophy, Truth was joined with Good and Beauty, so that passionate holding on to Truth would also translate into passionate holding on to the Good and the Beautiful, giving it aesthetic, axiological, and epistemological dimensions. King's association of this with love, and particularly with the beloved community that he developed at least partly in conversation with the work of Josiah Royce, is a tribute to the Greek milieu in which the Christian gospel was shaped. King saw Jesus as the embodiment of Truth ("I am the way, the truth, the life . . ."), and he extended this embodiment to the Church as a community identified with the body of Christ. Gandhi also picked up on this dimension of Christianity, combining it with his interpretation of the *Bhagavadgita*, which, as he read it, did not encourage participation in a war so much as it reminded both Arjuna and its readers never to confuse our partial vision with a vision of the whole. Gandhi's reminder of partial vision and King's equation of truth with love both provide considerable impetus toward community. We do not derive our power from an abstract community, but we need real encounter with other partial visions gathered in community as correctives to the distortion of our own. In King's theological language, this translates into a characteristically Protestant ecclesiology identified with a "beloved community" by which one may be embraced but to which one must choose to belong; but it is also a sociological vision in which, as later interpreters of King and of the personalist tradition have recognized, solidarity plays a critical role, and in which the parallel *polis* may be as important as formal structures in the constitution of authority.[1]

Necessity plays a key role in Ghandian philosophy of nonviolence, as, more generally, in ethics and political philosophy. More generally still, philosophy has taken Truth as necessary, non-contingent, and proceeded by distinguishing what is contingent from what is not. This is a critical point at which to identify both disagreements and formal agreement. Martin Luther King Jr. and Malcolm X, for example, converged philosophically on this question of "necessity," though it appears at first to separate them.[2] When Malcolm X repeated his now familiar "by any means necessary," he posed the necessary as both a practical and a philosophical question. This was a question of considerable interest to Gandhi and King, both of whom were inclined to King's conviction that the arc of the universe, though long, is toward justice. But King in particular acknowledged a healthy dose of neo-orthodox realism that kept him from being too sanguine about this. The point is that claims about what is necessary have an ontological force: this is the way the world is. In both Gandhi and King, this led to an understanding of means and ends that rejected violent means precisely because they would necessarily connect with violent ends. As long as violence is necessary, non-violence is not possible. Paradoxically, Malcolm articulated precisely this point in observations such as his much-criticized characterization of the assassination of John Kennedy as "the chickens coming home to roost." In the context of Gandhian philosophy, this is an accurate description of society permeated by violence: violence gives birth to violence. The puzzle this poses for a philosophy of nonviolence is whether nonviolence can possibly emerge from such a society. This, I think, is why Gandhi characterized *satyagraha* as an extension of the domestic law on the political field; and it is why Simone de Beauvoir associated ethics with ambiguity and resisted attempts to universalize it—an epistemological/ontological resistance she shared with Gandhi and King, one that she and

---

1. Isasi-Diaz, "Solidarity," 31–40. Havel, "Power of the Powerless," 23–96.
2. Cone, *Martin & Malcolm & America.*

King very likely derived from the same existentialist sources.[3] Violence is present in domestic affairs, but those affairs are permeated by nonviolence. Instances of violence stand out and demand notice; that they stand out is evidence that they are not the norm. This is why Gandhi said history is a record of violence and wars (these are the exceptional events that are recorded) and that a truly happy people would be one that had no history. And it is why Emma Goldman, for example, without justifying political violence, could understand it as an appropriately angry response to situations in which violence had become the norm—an observation that anticipates Malcolm's analysis and reaction to racism. When, early in his career and again almost exactly a year before his assassination, King turns to the social organization of nonviolence, he cultivates ground that he shares with Malcolm as well as with Jane Addams and Emma Goldman. Condemnation of violence is never an adequate response. An adequate response is one that constructs a city in which violence is not necessary—and that construction is an important point of controversy for political philosophy.

Remember: if violence is simply necessary, such a city is simply not possible. But if we are to live together in anything approaching a "beloved community," it is the possibility of such a city—and the task of building it—that will sustain our action.

Another way to proceed with regard to the important question of necessity is to examine structure in relation to construction and stability in relation to transformation. Without abandoning the category of necessity prematurely, we might shift our attention to structures that exhibit stability across time. One can observe, for example, that violent behavior is a stable feature of primate societies without claiming that violence is necessary in primate societies (or that it is a "natural" feature of all such societies). The difference this difference makes is that stability (unlike necessity) does not preclude change, but it lengthens our time frame.

Taking a snapshot (technically, a synchronic perspective, one that does not look into historical antecedents or developmental consequences) of primate (including human) interaction, is almost certain to reveal violent behavior. Take, for example, the front page of the *Chicago Tribune* on any given day. Two widely separated snapshots (a front page from, say, a hundred years ago and a front page from today) are not likely to differ

---

3. Erskine, *King Among the Theologians*. Vintges, *Philosophy as Passion*.

significantly in this regard (though we might want to make some observations about technological changes that have had an impact on levels of violence: clearly, our weapons are more destructive than they were a hundred years ago). In the evolutionary perspective adopted by Wrangham and Peterson, a hundred-year separation doesn't take us beyond the snapshot range: what we've really done in this case is highlighted two regions of the same snapshot.[4] They attempt a much wider separation, reaching as far back as ancestors common to all primates or (tightening the focus a little bit) common to chimpanzees and humans. They argue that violent behavior is present even in such widely separated snapshots and, more importantly, that what they refer to as "demonic" violence is associated with male primates even if the earlier snapshot is taken before the evolutionary split that divides humans from chimpanzees. Violent behavior associated with male primates exhibits substantial stability across time, and Wrangham and Peterson locate this stability in a process of adaptation that is associated with genetic predisposition.

Notice that they have introduced a new question here. Observing stability across two or more widely separated snapshots (you might as well go ahead and imagine twenty-four frames a second so the snapshots can be strung together into a moving picture, a diachronic perspective) raises the question of how stability is maintained across time. Wrangham and Peterson propose a perfectly respectable and plausible mechanism when they point to reproductive strategies associated with genetic transmission. From an evolutionary perspective, a behavior that demonstrates the kind of stability demonstrated by violence associated with male primates almost certainly has (or had) adaptive value. This violence (they argue) gave individuals in which it is observed a reproductive advantage at the same time that it either improved the likelihood of survival or at least did not interfere with survival of offspring who also exhibited it. This is not to argue that violent behavior (or violent behavior associated with male primates) made for "better" or even "stronger" primates. It's simply to argue that those primates had a better chance of reproducing (which sociobiologists suggest is the one thing genes are designed to do: the ones that do it well are more likely to survive than the ones that don't). Not surprisingly, a whole cascading cluster of effects would be associated with a process by which violent males gain a reproductive advantage over less

4. Wrangham and Peterson, *Demonic Males*.

violent males—and some of these effects would become apparent in social structures (which Wrangham and Peterson describe with reference particularly to chimpanzees, humans, and bonobos).

The bonobo reference marks another shift. Having noted that violent behavior associated with male primates is stable across time, Wrangham and Peterson examine a set of primate societies to compare how that violence interrelates with social structures. When they discover a primate society (bonobos) that (according to their reading of the data) has managed to control male violence, this is a cue to ask how. It's interesting that they do not look to genetics for the answer (or biological evolution), an important dimension, perhaps, in terms of time frame again. If we have to wait for primate evolution to take a turn away from male violence, we may have a long wait indeed. More likely, Wrangham and Peterson would suggest, we will never stop waiting, because it simply will not happen. They look instead to social organization and suggest that bonobos have developed social structures that keep male violence in check. If these cousins of ours can do it, they argue, perhaps we can as well. This is an interesting move, because it directs our attention to social structure and its interaction with evolutionary processes. Further, it suggests that our "wisdom" as well as our "intelligence" (a distinction by which they mean to highlight both memory and a capacity to project into the future) may allow us to intervene effectively in social transformation that addresses issues raised by "natural" processes. Recalling the snapshot metaphor, it is interesting to note that Wrangham and Peterson point toward a method that would diversify our snapshots in two directions—across time and across space. Just as they compare social structures observed in three primate species, we might effectively compare social structures observed within a single primate species: are some human social structures better able to hold violence in check than others? There's plenty of room for controversy in response to that question, but it suggests a potentially fruitful direction for research that could enable good argument as opposed to simple disputation. If the South African Truth and Reconciliation Commission appears to have worked better, for example, (or worse) than other institutions established after war (the Nuremberg Tribunals, perhaps? Reconstruction in the United States after the Civil War?), it might be worthwhile to ask why.

Regina Schwartz, too, takes a diachronic perspective, attending particularly to memory, identity, and culture as structures that demonstrate substantial stability across time and to narrative as the mechanism of their reproduction.[5] To put it simply, we are formed by our stories as surely as we form them. This is not a new observation (it certainly occurred to Plato when he proposed reining in poets in the society imaginatively constructed in his *Republic*), but that does not diminish its importance. One of the reasons human societies have consistently been so concerned about their stories is because those stories are a means by which the societies reproduce themselves. When Schwartz goes after stories associated with monotheism and rooted in Hebrew Scripture, it is at least in part because of the question posed by one of her students: "What about the Canaanites?" Returning to our snapshot metaphor, whether one takes a snapshot of the text or of the contemporary world, one can observe violent behavior rooted in the Exodus story. (And certainly this is not the only story where one can observe such behavior!) Schwartz suggests that we examine this more closely in at least two ways. First, we might ask whether some stories—or some ways of telling them—seem to be associated with less violence than others. If so, we might try to identify salient differences. In Hebrew Scripture (as Schwartz notes), we can find examples of both: consider Ruth, for example, which effectively undermines claims to exclusivity often associated with other books in the canon (such as Nehemiah). If we can tease out a complex interplay of stories rather than a monolithic narrative, we might be onto something. Second, we might ask after the possibility of new stories (as Salman Rushdie does, for example). Ruth may again serve as an example, since, by bringing an "outsider" in, it turns a narrative that is often taken to go "without saying" inside out. And there are others: consider the whole range of diaspora literatures in the postcolonial world—writers like Wole Soyinka, Ngugi wa Thiongo, Rushdie. Consider writers like Toni Morrison or Isabel Allende, who have begun to forge "new" stories out of the shards of old ones. John Sayles, too, belongs on this list as an artist who has attended carefully to memory and identity formation (as in his film *Lone Star*).

When Martha Reineke turns to Kristeva, women, and sacrifice, she gives us another variation to work with, one that is particularly concerned with structures of sacrifice.[6] I direct your attention to the end, where she writes of "an ethic of uncanny strangeness." So much of what Schwartz and Peterson/Wrangham discuss revolves around issues of territoriality and

---

5. Schwartz, *Curse of Cain.*
6. Reineke, *Sacrificed Lives.*

control—identifying "others" and keeping them "out" (or sucking them in). Reineke draws on Kristeva to suggest a shift of concern toward welcoming strangers (at least in part because we are strangers too—we "reside as strangers among strangers," she says). So much of our narrative production, social structure, and political behavior seems to have been directed over the years toward making ourselves at home and holding strangeness at bay that it may come as a shock to see strangeness held in such positive regard; but, as Frank Zappa said, "we are the other people." Taking that seriously enough to ask whether we can take it as a starting point for social/political transformation is an important step in the process of building the beloved community that was so central to King's thought.

Bibliography

Alanen, L. "Reconsidering Descartes' Notion of the Mind-Body Union." *Synthese* 106 (1996) 3–20.

Atherton, Margaret, editor. *Women Philosophers of the Early Modern Period*. Indianapolis: Hackett, 1994.

Auyang, Sunny Y. *How Is Quantum Field Theory Possible?* New York: Oxford University Press, 1995.

Baker, Houston A., Jr. "Blue Men, Black Writing, and Southern Revisions." In *Turning South Again: Re-thinking Modernism/Re-reading Booker T.*, 1–12. Durham, NC: Duke University Press, 2001.

Bateson, Gregory. "Cybernetic Explanation." *American Behavioral Scientist* 10:8 (1967) 29–32.

Beauvoir, Simone de. "The Positive Aspect of Ambiguity." In *The Ethics of Ambiguity*, 74–155. Translated by Bernard Frechtman. New York: Philosophical Library, 1948.

Bernal, Martin. *Black Athena: The Afroasiatic Roots of Classical Civilization*. Piscataway, NJ: Rutgers University Press, 1994.

Blom, John J., translator. *Descartes, His Moral Philosophy and Psychology*. New York: New York University Press, 1978.

Boulton, Alexander O. "The American Paradox: Jeffersonian Equality and Racial Science." *American Quarterly* 47 (1995) 467–92.

Brooks, Van Wyck. "On Creating a Usable Past." *Dial* (April 1918) 337–41.

Brown, Stuart. "Leibniz and More's Cabbalistic Circle." In *Henry More (1614–1687) Tercentenary Studies*, edited by Sarah Hutton, 77–96. Dordrecht: Kluwer Academic, 1990.

Bynum, Caroline Walker. *The Resurrection of the Body in Western Christianity, 200–1336*. New York: Columbia University Press, 1995.

Chomsky, Noam. Interview on Radio B92, Belgrade. September 19, 2001. Online: http://www.b92.net/intervju/eng/2001/0919-chomsky.html.

Cohn-Sherbock, Dan. *The Crucified Jew: Twenty Centuries of Christian Anti-Semitism*. Grand Rapids: Eerdmans, 1997.

Coleridge, Samuel Taylor. *Biographia Literaria*. Edited by James Engell and W. Jackson Bate. Princeton University Press, 1983.

Cone, James H. *Martin & Malcolm & America: A Dream or a Nightmare*. Maryknoll, NY: Orbis, 1991.

Conway, Anne. *Principles of the Most Ancient and Modern Philosophy*. Edited by Peter Loptson. The Hague: Martinus Nijhoff, 1982.

———. *The Principles of the Most Ancient and Modern Philosophy*. Translated by Allison P. Coudert and Taylor Corse. Cambridge: Cambridge University Press, 1996.

Crocker, Robert. "Henry More: A Biographical Essay." In *Henry More (1614–1687) Tercentenary Studies*, edited by Sarah Hutton, 1–18. Dordrecht: Kluwer Academic, 1990.

Crossan, John Dominic. *Who Killed Jesus?: Exposing the Roots of Anti-Semitism in the Gospel Story of the Death of Jesus*. San Francisco: HarperSanFrancisco, 1995.

cummings, e. e. "somewhere i have never travelled, gladly beyond." In *Complete Poems: 1904–1962*. New York: Liveright, 1991.

Cunneen, Sally. *In Search of Mary: The Woman and the Symbol*. New York: Ballantine, 1996.

Curd, P. K. "Eleatic Monism in Zeno and Melissus." *Ancient Philosophy* 13 (1993) 1–22.

Debray, Regis. *Media Manifestos: On the Technological Transmission of Cultural Forms*. Translated by Eric Rauth. New York: Verso, 1996.

Deleuze, Gilles. *The Fold: Leibniz and the Baroque*. Translated by Tom Conley. New York: Continuum, 2006.

Descartes, René. *Meditations on First Philosophy*. Translated by Donald A. Cress. Indianapolis: Hackett, 1979.

Dillard, Annie. "Teaching a Stone to Talk." In *Teaching a Stone to Talk*, 67–76. New York: Harper & Row, 1983.

Duran, Jane. "Anne Viscountess Conway: A Seventeenth Century Rationalist." *Hypatia* 4 (1989) 64–79.

Equiano, Olaudah. *The Interesting Narrative and Other Writings*. Edited with an introduction and notes by Vincent Carretta. New York: Penguin, 1995.

Erskine, Noel Leo. *King Among the Theologians*. Cleveland: Pilgrim, 1994.

Fletcher, Richard A. *The Barbarian Conversion: From Paganism to Christianity*. Berkeley: University of California Press, 1999.

Frank, Isnard Wilhelm. *A Concise History of the Mediaeval Church*. Translated by John Bowden. London: Continuum, 1995.

Fredriksen, Paula. *From Jesus to Christ: The Origins of the New Testament Images of Jesus*. 2nd ed. New Haven: Yale University Press, 2000.

Freeman, Kathleen. *Ancilla to the Presocratic Philosophers*. Cambridge: Harvard University Press, 1983.

Friedman, Richard E. *The Disappearance of God: A Divine Mystery*. Boston: Little, Brown, 1995.

Gabbey, Alan. "Henry More and the Limits of Mechanism." In *Henry More (1614–1687) Tercentenary Studies*, edited by Sarah Hutton, 19–35. Dordrecht: Kluwer Academic, 1990.

Gager, John G. *Reinventing Paul*. New York: Oxford University Press, 2000.

Gandhi, Mahatma K. "What Styagraha Is." In *Non-Violent Resistance*, 3–36. New York: Schocken, 1951.

Gibson, J. J. *The Ecological Approach to Visual Perception*. Boston: Houghton, 1979.

Ginzburg, Carlo. *The Cheese and the Worms: The Cosmos of a Sixteenth Century Miller*. Translated by John Tedeschi and Anne Tedeschi. Baltimore: Johns Hopkins University Press, 1992.

Goldman, Emma. "The Psychology of Political Violence." In *Anarchism and Other Essays*, 79–108. New York: Dover, 1969.

Grosholz, Emily. "Plato and Leibniz against the Materialists." *Journal of the History of Ideas* 57 (1996) 255–76.

Hansen, Chad. *A Daoist Theory of Chinese Thought: A Philosopohical Interpretation.* Oxford: Oxford University Press, 1992.

Havel, Václav. "The Power of the Powerless." In *The Power of the Powerless*, 23–96. Armonk, NY: Sharpe, 1995.

Hilbert, David. "On the infinite." In *From Frege to Gödel: A Source Book in Mathematical Logic, 1879–1931*, edited by Jean van Heijenoort, 367–92. Cambridge: Harvard University Press, 1967.

Hofstadter, Douglas R. *Gödel, Escher, Bach: An Eternal Golden Braid.* New York: Basic, 1979.

Hopkins, Keith. *A World Full of Gods: The Strange Triumph of Christianity.* New York: Free, 2000.

Hountondji, Paulin J. *African Philosophy: Myth and Reality.* 2nd ed. Bloomington: Indiana University Press, 1996.

Hyland, D. A. "Potentiality and Presence in Plato: The Significance of Place in the Platonic Dialogues." *Journal of Speculative Philosophy* 8 (1994) 28–43.

Isasi-Diaz, Ada Maria. "Solidarity: Love of Neighbor in the 1980s." In *Lift Every Voice: Constructing Christian Theologies from the Underside*, edited by Susan Brooks Thistlethwaite and Mary Potter Engel, 31–40. New York: Harper & Row, 1990.

Jefferson, Thomas. *Notes on the State of Virginia.* Edited by William Peden. New York: 1954 (1785).

Kee, Howard Clark. *Who Are the People of God? Early Christian Models of Community.* New Haven: Yale University Press, 1995.

King, Martin Luther, Jr. "The Social Organization of Nonviolence" (1959) and "A Time To Break Silence" (1967). In *A Testament of Hope: The Essential Writings of Martin Luther King, Jr.*, edited by James Melvin, 31–34 and 231–44. San Francisco: Harper & Row, 1986.

Kirk, Geoffrey, John Earle Raven, and Malcolm Schofield. *The Presocratic Philosophers: A Critical History with a Selection of Texts.* 2nd ed. New York: Cambridge University Press, 1983.

Leibniz, G. W. *Philosophischen Schriften.* Edited by C. F. Gerhardt. Hildesheim: Georg Olms, 1960.

Lloyd, Genevieve. *The Man of Reason: Male and Female in Western Philosophy.* 2nd ed. London: Routledge, 1993.

Locke, John. *An Essay Concerning Human Understanding.* New York: Barnes, 2004.

Lüdemann, Gerd. *Heretics: The Other Side of Early Christianity.* Translated by John Bowden. Louisville: Wetminster John Knox, 1996.

Luther, Martin. "Lecture on Galatians." In *Martin Luther's Basic Theological Writings*, edited by Timothy Lull, 18–24. Minneapolis: Fortress, 2005.

MacKinnon, Flora Isabel. *Philosophical Writings of Henry More.* Oxford: Oxford University Press, 1925.

Mandelbrot, Benoit. *The Fractal Geometry of Nature.* New York: Freeman, 1983.

Marable, Manning. "Structural Racism and American Democracy: Historical and Theoretical Perspectives." *Souls* 3 (2001) 6–24.

McKeon, Richard. *Introduction to Aristotle.* New York: Modern Library, 1947.

Merchant, Carolyn. *The Death of Nature.* San Francisco: Harper, 1989.

Merleau-Ponty, Maurice. *Phenomenology of Perception.* Translated by Colin Smith. New York: Humanities, 1962.

Morrison, Toni. *Beloved: A Novel.* New York: Knopf, 2006.

———. "The Site of Memory." In *Out There: Marginalization and Contemporary Cultures,* edited by Russell Ferguson, Martha Gever, Trinh T. Minh-ha, and Cornel West, 299–305. Boston: MIT Press, 1990.

O'Connor, Flannery. "Some Aspects of the Grotesque in Southern Fiction." In *Mystery and Manners,* 36–50. New York: Farrar, Straus & Giroux, 1961.

Olela, Henry. "The African Foundations of Greek Philosophy." In *African Philosophy: An Anthology,* edited by Emmanuel Chukwudi Eze, 43–49. London: Blackwell, 1998.

Reineke, Martha J. *Sacrificed Lives: Kristeva on Women and Violence.* Bloomington: Indiana University Press, 1997.

Rich, Adrienne. "Vesuvius at Home: The Power of Emily Dickinson." In *On Lies, Secrets, and Silence: Selected Prose 1966–1978,* 151–83. New York: Norton, 1979.

Ricoeur, Paul. *Time and Narrative.* Vol. I. Translated by Kathleen McLaughlin and David Pellauer. Chicago: University of Chicago Press, 1984.

Rubenstein, Richard E. *When Jesus Became God: The Epic Struggle Over Christ's Divinity in the Last Days of Rome.* New York: Houghton Mifflin, 1999.

Rushdie, Salman. "The Location of Brazil." In *Imaginary Homelands,* 118–25. New York: Penguin, 1991.

Russell, Bertrand. *The Philosophy of Leibniz: With an Appendix of Leading Passages.* London: Routledge, 1992.

Salisbury, Joyce E. *Perpetua's Passion: The Death and Memory of a Young Roman Woman.* London: Routledge, 1997.

Schwartz, Regina M. *The Curse of Cain: The Violent Legacy of Monotheism.* Chicago: University of Chicago Press, 1997.

Shipman, Pat. *The Evolution of Racism.* New York: Simon & Schuster, 1994.

Shirley, Samuel, translator. *Spinoza, The Ethics and Selected Letters.* Indianapolis: Hackett, 1982.

Spinoza, Benedictus de. *The Essential Spinoza: Ethics and Related Writings.* Translated by Samuel Shirley. Indianapolis: Hackett, 2006.

Taylor, Mark C. "Unsettling Issues." *Journal of the American Academy of Religion* 62 (1994) 949–63.

Thoreau, Henry David. "On Civil Disobedience" (1849). In *Walden and Civil Disobedience.* New York: Harper, 1965.

Vintges, Karen. *Philosophy as Passion: The Thinking of Simone de Beauvoir.* Bloomington: Indiana University Press, 1996.

Vonnegut, Kurt. *Slaughterhouse-five: Or, The Children's Crusade, a Duty-dance with Death.* New York: Delacorte, 1969.

Walker, Alice. "Beyond the Peacock: The Reconstruction of Flannery O'Connor." In *In Search of Our Mothers' Gardens,* 42–59. New York: Harcourt, 1983.

Walker, David. *David Walker's Appeal.* Boston: n.p., 1830.

Welch, Sharon D. *Sweet Dreams in America.* London: Routledge, 1999.

West, Cornel. "A Genealogy of Modern Racism." In *Prophesy Deliverance: An Afro-American Revolutionary Christianity,* 47–65. Philadelphia: Westminster, 1982.

Winch, Peter. "Mind, Body & Ethics in Spinoza." *Philosophical Investigations* 18 (1995) 216–34.

Woolf, Virginia. *Flush: A Biography.* New York: Hogarth, 1933.

Wrangham, Richard, and Dale Peterson. *Demonic Males: Apes and the Origins of Human Violence.* New York: Houghton Mifflin, 1996.

Index